A BEGINNER'S HANDBOOK TO BIBLICAL HEBREW

A BEGINNER'S HANDBOOK TO BIBLICAL HEBREW

John H. Marks
and
Virgil M. Rogers

ABINGDON PRESS

NASHVILLE NEW YORK

A BEGINNER'S HANDBOOK TO BIBLICAL HEBREW

Standard Book Number: 687-02616-4
Library of Congress Catalog Card Number: 58-7434

PRINTED AND BOUND BY THE PARTHENON PRESS AT NASHVILLE, TENNESSEE, UNITED STATES OF AMERICA

INTRODUCTION

The teaching of the Word of God in the original languages should be of perennial interest, especially for the minister who wishes to unfold the riches of the Bible. In too many instances, however, Hebrew has been taught as though it actually were a "dead" language, and this attitude has been reflected in the methods of instruction employed. Consequently, the results of teaching Hebrew in theological seminaries have frequently been very disappointing. Sometimes so many grammatical details were presented that the student never had an opportunity of covering any ground in reading the language. In other cases, for the sake of minimizing the labor of the student, Hebrew was not taught systematically, and in consequence the difficulty of the tongue was increased and in the end the student became discouraged or bewildered. It was said that the theological student would use Hebrew only for exegetical purposes or for making word studies in order to find theological conceptions. By this method, however, the student never got a grasp of the language, and from the very beginning he was defeated in his purpose of using Hebrew for exegesis. Those teachers overlooked the fact that word studies and expositions based on the original demand the ability to enter into the spirit of the language of the Bible. The great ideas of the Old Testament are enshrined in words, and the key to them is found in a working knowledge of Hebrew.

Great advances have been made in recent years in the teaching of modern languages, and teachers of Hebrew can gain by these pedagogical improvements.

The language of the Old Testament throbs with life, and under proper methods of instruction students can develop a feeling for the tongue of ancient Israel.

The authors of this grammar, my former students, who are now my colleagues in Princeton, had a scientific training in Semitic languages, but at the same time they retained a practical outlook. By using a combination of the inductive and deductive method, they begin the reading of Genesis very early in the course in Elementary Hebrew, and during the year students acquire definite grammatical principles, a basic vocabulary, and the ability to read Biblical Hebrew. The authors are to be commended for having made available in book form the results of their experience and for giving a wider public the benefit of their achievements.

Henry S. Gehman

Princeton Theological Seminary
and
Princeton University
June 1, 1956

PREFACE

This book is written for students interested in Biblical Hebrew. It aims at giving them both an introductory text and a book for future reference, not an exhaustive grammar. The book is therefore neither strictly a textbook nor a grammatical treatise, but rather a handbook for ready reference.

The authors are convinced that a working knowledge of Hebrew is essential to understanding the Old Testament. Students, they have observed, either do not grasp the relevance of grammatical study for their future ministry or else are subjected to an oversimplified grammatical training which does not equip them to make practical use of their knowledge in the study of the Old Testament. Hoping to avoid the extremes of bewildering details and obscure oversimplification, and at the same time to present an interesting and complete grammatical treatment, the writers have presumed to add their text to the increasing number of Hebrew grammars already available.

The approach is both deductive and inductive. Primary elements of grammar are introduced slowly, to which more difficult principles are gradually added. Nothing new is introduced which either cannot be deduced from earlier fundamental points or is not explained at once. The arrangement thus progresses slowly but firmly toward the minimal requirements for reading Biblical Hebrew. At the same time, however, readings from Genesis are added, both to heighten interest in learning grammar and to provide the ground for inductive study.

Examples illustrating grammatical principles are, when possible, taken from Genesis; the vocabularies are from Genesis, and a section of notes to the beginning chapters of Genesis is included. These are meant as simple aids to the mastery of the language, to give students a reference for simple points not easily found elsewhere. For the same reason complete paradigms are included, so that students may "see in print" the correct appearance of any form, whether it actually occurs in the Old Testament or not.

One of the aims in writing this book has been to provide a manual for self-instruction. To this end numerous helps have been provided. But the goal has also been to encourage students to buy the standard lexicons and the grammar of Gesenius-Kautzsch. The authors, therefore, have attempted to make this manual as complete as possible for the beginner. The student may then, without duplicating elementary books which would have been necessary for his beginning days, purchase the expensive but vital aids to his further study of the Old Testament.

The authors gratefully acknowledge the encouragement and help of Professor H.S. Gehman of Princeton Theological Seminary, who not only read the entire manuscript and offered valuable suggestions, but also gave permission for the use of the mimeographed manuscript as the grammar for beginning Hebrew at Princeton Seminary. The authors are also indebted to Professors C.T. Fritsch and D.H. Gard, who used the mimeographed text and offered helpful criticisms. Professor G.A. Barrois kindly read the entire manuscript and made constructive suggestions, for which the authors are grateful. Special acknowledgment must also be made of the help in clarifying difficult points received from the grammars of Bauer-Leander, Bergsträsser, Gesenius-Kautzsch, and Hollenberg-Budde, edited by W. Baumgartner.

J.M.
V.R.

Princeton, New Jersey
May 1956

The mimeographed edition has been carefully revised during two years of use at Princeton Theological Seminary. For helpful suggestions in revision the authors are grateful to Professor J.H. Macrae, who used this grammar as the text for beginning Hebrew at Union Theological Seminary, Richmond, Virginia. The entire manuscript was typed for publication by Willard Gurdon Oxtoby, a graduate student at Princeton University, whose assistance in the preparation of the format was invaluable.

November 1957

TABLE OF CONTENTS

To the Student

This grammar is designed to be used in conjunction with the text of Genesis, and all biblical references unless otherwise noted refer to Genesis. The arrangement of the material, however, is not dependent upon any sequence of grammatical difficulty in Genesis. The grammar, therefore, may be used with any biblical text, but the section "Words, Meanings, References to Grammar" would not then be applicable.

The student must first master the elements of orthography to the point where he can read aloud ten or twelve verses of Hebrew text with rapidity and ease. Beginning with the study of the article he is ready to start translating. The section "Words, Meanings, References to Grammar" may then be used to guide him through the difficulties of the text while he at the same time learns grammar deductively. Thus he translates and bypasses grammatical points which he has not yet learned, and when he encounters in his deductive learning the material bypassed, its relevance becomes apparent. His completion of the grammar should roughly coincide with the translation of three chapters of Genesis.

The section "Words, Meanings, References to Grammar" lists all new words from Genesis 1 through 22 as they occur.

PART I

§1. Consonants

Hebrew consonant	Pronunciation of Hebrew name	Hebrew name
א	Ah´-lĕf	ʾĀlep̱
ב	Beyth (ey as in 'they')	Bêṯ
ג	Gĭ´-mĕl (g, ĭ, as in 'go,' 'hit')	Gimel
ד	Dah´-lĕth	Dāleṯ
ה	Hay	Hê
ו	Wow (ow as in 'owl')	Wāw
ז	Ză´-yĭn	Zayin
ח	Cheyth (ch as in Scot. 'loch' or German 'machen')	Ḥêṯ
ט	Teyth	Ṭêṯ
י	Yothe (othe as in 'clothe')	Yôḏ
כ	Kăf (as in 'caffeine')	Kap̱
ל	Lah´-mĕth (th as in 'wither')	Lāmeḏ
מ	Meym (rhymes with 'same')	Mêm
נ	Noon	Nûn
ס	Sah´-mĕk	Sāmeḵ
ע	ʿĂ´-yĭn	ʿAyin
פ	Pay	Pê
צ	Ṣah´-the (th as in 'them')	Ṣāḏê
ק	Qof (o as in 'note')	Qôp̱
ר	Reysh	Rêš
שׂ	Seen	Śîn
שׁ	Sheen	Šîn
ת	Tou (ou as in 'out')	Tāw

Notes to pronunciation: ă as in 'fat,' ĕ as in 'met,' ĭ as in 'fit,' ah as the a in 'father,'

Trans-literation	Approximate pronunciation value of Hebrew consonant	Form of consonant at end of word only
ʾ	Glottal stop as initial sound in 'apple.' Initial sound of escaping breath before vowel is sounded.	
b̲	v, as in 'vest'	
g̲	g, as in 'wagon'	
d̲	th, as in 'then' or 'wither'	
h	h, as in 'hat'	
w	w, as in 'way'	
z	z, as in 'zone'	
ḥ	ch, as in Scot. 'loch' or German 'machen'	
ṭ	t explosive	
y	y, as in 'yes'	
k̲	ch, as in German 'ich'	ך
l	l, as in 'lay'	
m	m, as in 'may'	ם
n	n, as in 'nay'	ן
s	s, as in 'say'	
ʿ	A guttural sound made by tightening the throat and exploding breath	
p̲	ph, as in 'phonic'	ף
ṣ	c, as in 'princess' (explosive s)	ץ
q	q, as in 'mosque'	
r	r, as in 'rat'	
ś	s, as in 'say'	
š	sh, as in 'shine'	
t̲	th, as in 'think'	

ey as in 'they'

1. Formation of consonants:

Hebrew is written from right to left.

To form the letters, begin with the upper left corner. All consonants except ל, ק, and final ך, ן, ף, and ץ when written properly can be placed into a square. ל is the only consonant which extends above the square; ק and final ך, ן, ף, ץ extend below the square.

Note: The following consonants should be carefully distinguished:

ב and כ	ה, ח and ת
ו, ז and נ, ן	final ם and ס
ד, ר and ה	ע and צ

2. The following consonants are called laryngeals: א, ה, ח, ע, and sometimes ר.

Note: Column 2 of the table is merely an aid to pronunciation; the student must memorize column 3.

§2. <u>Consonants with Two Pronunciations</u>. <u>The Dāg̲ēš Lēnē</u>

Dāg̲ēš lēnē (dah΄-gĕsh ley΄-ney) is a dot placed within the consonants ב, ג, ד, כ, פ, ת. These six consonants (which may be remembered by the mnemonic word 'Bega<u>d</u>kepa<u>t</u>'), which in the table are underlined in transliteration (column 4) have a soft pronunciation (spirant) when they appear without dāg̲ēš. They also have a hard pronunciation (stop) which is indicated by the dāg̲ēš lēnē. Thus:

בּ	Pronounced	b	as in	'boy,'	transliterated	b
גּ	"	g	" "	'go,'	"	g
דּ	"	d	" "	'dog,'	"	d
כּ	"	k	" "	'kit,'	"	k
פּ	"	p	" "	'pin,'	"	p
תּ	"	t	" "	'toy,'	"	t

Note 1: Distinguish between the transliteration and pronunciation of these six consonants when they are written with and without dāg̱ēš lēnē.

בּ, b; ב, ḇ
גּ, g; ג, g̱
דּ, d; ד, ḏ
כּ, k; כ, ḵ
פּ, p; פ, p̱
תּ, t; ת, ṯ

Note 2: These six consonants are spirants (i.e., have no dāg̱ēš lēnē) when they are preceded by a vowel. Observe the g̱, ḏ, p̱, ṯ in 'Be-g̱aḏkep̱aṯ.'

Note 3: The dāg̱ēš forte is a dot within a consonant (except laryngeals) to show that it is doubled, e.g., הַשָּׁמַיִם haš-šā-ma'-yim 1:1. The dāg̱ēš forte will be further explained in §9.

§3. <u>Vowel Signs</u>

Sign	Pronunciation of Hebrew name	Hebrew name	Trans-literation	Approximate* pronunciation value of Hebrew sign
ָ	Qah́-mĕss	Qāmeṣ	ā	as a in 'father'
ַ	Pắ-thăch	Paṯaḥ	a	as a in 'fat'
ֵ	Seý-rey	Ṣērē	ē	as ey in 'they'
ֶ	Se-goaĺ (s^e as se in 'serene')	S^{e}ḡôl	e	as e in 'met'
ִ	Chí-rĕq	Ḥîreq	i	as i in 'hit'
ֹ	Chó-lĕm	Ḥōlem	ō	as o in 'note'
ָ	Qah́-mĕss chah-toof́	Qāmeṣ ḥāṭûp	o	as o in 'gone'
ֻ	Qĭb-boosś	Qibbûṣ	u	as u in 'put'

Note 1: The vowel signs except ḥōlem stand under the consonant after which they are pronounced, e.g., דָּבָר dā-ḇār.

Note 2: The ḥōlem appears at the upper left corner of the consonant which it follows, e.g., תֹהוּ 1:2. When ḥōlem (˙) precedes Šîn (שׁ) it coalesces with the dot of the Šîn, e.g., חֹשֶׁךְ 1:2. When ḥōlem follows Śîn (שׂ) it coalesces with the dot of the Śîn, e.g., שֹׂנֵא. When ḥōlem precedes Śîn or follows Šîn, the consonant appears with two dots, e.g., עֹשֶׂה ʿō-śe(h) 1:11; שֹׁפֵט šō-pēṭ; לִמְשֹׁל 1:18. The Kittel text of the Old Testament uses two dots in all instances and does not follow this rule.

Note 3: The student will observe that qāmeṣ and

---

*The Hebrew pure vowel is not adequately represented by English vowel sounds; e.g., o in 'note' and ey in 'they' are really diphthongs.

qāmes hātûp are written alike; he is unable at this point to distinguish between them. The first occurrence of qāmeṣ ḥāṭûp̱ is in 1:21 כָּל, which also occurs in verses 25, 26, 29, and 30. It also occurs in 1:29 in לְאָכְלָה leʾoḵlâ. The distinction will be made clear after the student has been introduced to syllabic structure. Cf. §11.2.

§4. Vowel Letters

Originally Hebrew had no written vowels; the following consonants, however, were often used to indicate long vowels: א, ה, ו, י. When the Masoretes introduced their vowel signs, they added their signs to these consonants.

Sign	Pronunciation of Hebrew name	Hebrew name	Trans-liter-ation	Pronunciation value of Hebrew sign
ִי	Chí-rĕq yothe	Ḥîreq Yôḏ	î	as i in 'machine'
וֹ	Chó-lĕm wow	Ḥōlem Wāw	ô	as o in 'note'
ֵי	Séy-rey yothe	Ṣērē Yôḏ	ê	as ey in 'they'
וּ	Shoó-rĕq	Šûreq	û	as u in 'sure'
ָה	Qáh-mĕss hay	Qāmeṣ Hê	â	as a in 'father'

Note 1: Full and defective writing:

When the originally long vowel is written with its vowel letter, it is written fully (plena); this is called full writing (scriptio plena). When the vowel letter is omitted it is written defectively (defectiva); this is called defective writing (scriptio defectiva).

וֹ may appear ֹ מְאֹרֹת for מְאוֹרוֹת 1:14
ִי may appear ִ הַתַּנִּנִם for הַתַּנִּינִים 1:21
וּ may appear ֻ וְכִבְשֻׁהָ for וְכִבְשׁוּהָ 1:28

The following consonants lose their consonantal value and coalesce with the preceding vowel according to the following table:

Combination	Transliteration	Pronunciation value
אָ	ā᾽	as a in 'father'
אֵ	ē᾽	as ey in 'they'
אֶ	e᾽	as e in 'met'
אֹ	ō᾽	as o in 'note'
הֵ	ē(h)	as ey in 'they'
הֶ	e(h)	as e in 'met'
הֹ	ō(h)	as o in 'note'
יֶ	e(y)	as e in 'met'

Note 2: All ᾽Aleps in the above table are transliterated but not pronounced; in transliteration they are written to preserve the original spelling.

Mappîq: When final ה is consonantal rather than vocalic, a dot called mappîq is placed within it, e.g., הּ as in לְמִינָהּ l^{e}mînāh 1:24.

§5. Classification of Vowels

There are three original Semitic vowels: a, i, u. In Hebrew they are inflected as follows:

	a	i	u
Short	ַ or ֶ	ִ or ֶ	ֻ or ָ (qāmeṣ ḥāṭûp)
Lengthened	ָ (qāmeṣ)	ֵ	•

Note: Short and lengthened vowels may change because of accentual conditions. The vowels ḥîreq yôḏ, ḥōlem wāw, ṣērē yôḏ, šûreq, and qāmeṣ hê are originally long and do not change.

§6. Patah Furtive

Whenever the laryngeals ה, ח, ע, are final and are preceded by a long vowel other than the "a" type, a pataḥ, known as pataḥ furtive, appears between the vowel and the final consonant as an aid to pronunciation. This pataḥ furtive is written underneath the final consonant but is pronounced before it, e.g., רוּחַ 1:2; רָקִיעַ 1:6; מַזְרִיעַ 1:11. These words are transliterated: rû(a)ḥ, rāqî(a)ʿ, mazrî(a)ʿ. The pataḥ furtive is merely an aid to pronunciation and does not have syllabic value.

§7. Syllabic Structure

1. Every syllable in Hebrew must begin with one consonant, i.e., a vowel cannot begin a syllable (the single exception, as in וּבֵין û-ḇên 1:4, will be considered later).
2. Kinds of syllables:
   a. Open: ends with a vowel or a vowel with its vowel letter. Cf. the table in §4. בָּרָא bā-rā' 1:1 (open syllables).
   b. Closed: ends with a consonant. בְּרֵאשִׁית bᵉ-rē'-šîṯ 1:1 (the final syllable is closed).

§8. The Šᵉwā'

The name 'šᵉwā'' (שְׁוָא, hereafter written 'shewa') is pronounced sh-wah́, its vowels being similar in pronunciation to the successive vowels in 'the wasp.'

The shewa is represented by the sign (ְ) as in בְּרֵאשִׁית 1:1.

There are two types:

1. Vocal. This shewa, which has a slight vocalic sound, is not a full vowel. It may be called

a half-vowel because of its extremely short
pronunciation, as the "e" in the expression
'the wasp.' וְאֵת; בְּרֵאשִׁית 1:1

a. The vocal shewa may be regarded as the expression of an original vowel. A consonant with vocal shewa is usually regarded as a part of the following syllable,
   but since the shewa represents an original vowel the consonant with which it
   occurs will be treated in this grammar
   as an open syllable.

b. The vocal shewa is transliterated by a
   small e above the line, e.g., בְּ b^e.

c. Appearing chiefly under laryngeals are
   three different compound (vocalic) shewas which are indicated by writing the
   signs of the three short vowels pat̲aḥ,
   s^eg̲ôl, qāmeṣ ḥāṭûp, to the left of the
   simple shewa, thus: ֲ ֱ ֳ . These
   compound shewas are called respectively
   ḥāṭēp̲-pat̲aḥ, ḥāṭēp̲-seg̲ôl, and ḥāṭēp̲-qā-
   meṣ. They are transliterated:

   ֲ small a above the line, e.g., אֲשֶׁר
   ʾašer 1:7.

   ֱ small e with breve above the line,
   e.g., אֱלֹהִים ^eʾlôhîm 1:1. Cf. §4, note
   1 (defective ḥōlem).

   ֳ small o above the line, e.g., חֳלִי
   ḥ^olî.

   The compound shewa is slightly differen-
   tiated in pronunciation from the simple
   vocal shewa in that it is pronounced
   with the slight coloring of the corresponding short vowel.

2. _Silent_. This shewa is used within a word to
   indicate the end of a _closed_ syllable. וַיִּקְרָא

1:5. Normally the silent shewa is not used at the end of a word; i.e., it is used under the last consonant of a closed syllable which is not final in the word. Silent shewa is not transliterated.

The vowel preceding silent shewa is always short unless accented.

Note 1: Two vocal shewas never occur together. When two shewas occur together, the first is always silent, e.g., יִשְׁרְצוּ 1:20.

Note 2: A shewa at the beginning of a word is always vocal, e.g., תְּהוֹם 1:2.

Note 3: A vowelless final kap̱ (ךְ) carries a sign like a silent shewa to distinguish it from final nûn (ן). חֹשֶׁךְ 1:2.

Note 4: The vowel letters when quiescent do not take a silent shewa, since they do not close a syllable. Cf. §4. בְּרֵאשִׁית 1:1.

Note 5: Shewa medium. The shewa medium is classed either as vocal or silent because it loosely closes the syllable to which it belongs and thus does not permit a following begaḏkep̱aṯ consonant to take dāḡēš lēnē, e.g., רִדְפוּ, מַלְכֵי, בִּדְבַר. This shewa may be read as either silent or vocal. The shewa medium is a peculiar phenomenon which the beginning student should simply observe but not attempt to explain.

§9. Dāḡēš Forte

The dāḡēš forte is a dot within a consonant (except laryngeals) to show that it is doubled, e.g., הַשָּׁמַיִם haš-šā-ma'-yim 1:1; הַמָּיִם ham-mā'-yim 1:2; וַיֹּאמֶר way-yō'-mer 1:3.

Dāḡēš forte and dāḡēš lēnē are distinguished as follows:

1. Dāgēš forte is always preceded by a full vowel, never by vocal shewa.
2. Dāgēš lēnē is never preceded by a vowel or vocal shewa; it is preceded within a word by silent shewa, e.g., וַיַּבְדֵּל 1:4.

Note 1: The student will observe that a dot in a begadkepat consonant may be either dāgēš lēnē or dāgēš forte. The pronunciation in either instance is hard, e.g., דִּבֵּר dibbēr.

A begadkepat letter at the beginning of a word regularly takes dāgēš lēnē; if, however, an immediately preceding word ends in a vowel, this dāgēš lēnē may be dropped, e.g., פְּנֵי תְהוֹם 1:2.

If a shewa stands under a letter bearing dāgēš lēnē or dāgēš forte, it is always vocal. A shewa following an unaccented short vowel is normally silent.

Note 2: Within a word a closed syllable whose final consonant bears dāgēš forte is called a sharpened syllable, e.g., הַשָּׁמַיִם haš-šā-ma′-yim 1:1.

Note 3: Euphonic dāgēš: Doubling often occurs for euphonic reasons. עֹשֶׂה פְּרִי 1:11; אֶעֱשֶׂה־לּוֹ 2:18; לְקֳחָה־זֹּאת 2:23.

§10. Summary of Rules for Recognition of Silent and Vocal Shewa

1. Initial shewa is always vocal.
2. Final shewa is always silent.
3. Medial shewa is:
   a. Silent
      1) When preceded by a short unaccented vowel.
      2) When followed by a consonant with dāgēš.

3) When followed by a consonant with shewa.

b. Vocal

1) When preceded by meteg.

2) When the consonant under which it appears bears dāgēš.

§11. Word Accent (Tone)

1. Every Hebrew word has one primary accent which usually occurs on the final syllable, the ultima. An ultimate accent is not indicated in this grammar. When the primary accent is not on the last syllable, it will be noted by the mûnaḥ (֣). קָטַ֣לְתָּ.

2. Meteg: a small vertical line placed to the left of the vowel sign to indicate a secondary word accent, e.g., הָֽיְתָה 1:2. Meteg will occur, when necessary, on the second syllable before the primary accent.

Note: The student will observe that meteg placed before a shewa indicates that the shewa is vocal. Distinguish חָכְמָה and חָֽכְמָה, ḥokmâ and ḥākemâ. Observe further; qāmeṣ ḥāṭûp occurs only in a closed unaccented syllable or in an open syllable before ֳ, e.g., בָּֽחֳלִי boḥoli.

3. Maqqēp: a horizontal line placed between two words, binding them together into one accentual unit. The primary accent falls on the final word, e.g., וַֽיְהִי־אוֹר 1:3; כִּי־טוֹב 1:4.

§12. The Accent Signs

The accents in Hebrew serve a threefold purpose:

1. They indicate word accent (tone). Cf. §11.

2. They regulate the chanting of Scripture in the

Synagogue.

3. They serve as marks of punctuation. As punctuation marks they may be disjunctive (separa-
ting) or conjunctive (joining).

Of the thirty-odd accents used in the Old
Testament, two disjunctive accents must be
learned at this point.

   a. ꞌAtnāḥ: (ˏ), e.g., אֱלֹהִ֑ים 1:1. This accent marks the principal division within the
verse; it always falls on the accented syllable of the word under which it occurs.

   b. Sillûq: This accent, which cannot be distinguished in appearance from the meteg, always appears under the accented syllable of
the last word in each verse. This word is
followed immediately by Sôp̱ Pasûq (:), which
ends the verse. הָאָֽרֶץ׃ 1:1

Pause: A syllable which receives the accents
ꞌatnāḥ (ˏ) or sillûq (ˌ), and sometimes others, is said to be in pause. The accented
short vowel of a word in pause may change to
the corresponding lengthened vowel, e.g., מַ֫יִם
לָמָֽיִם׃ 1:6.

§13. Peculiarities of the Laryngeals

The laryngeals, א, ה, ח, ע, and sometimes ר:
1. Reject dāḡēš forte.

   a. א, ע, and ר, by rejecting dāḡēš forte,
normally cause the preceding vowel to be
lengthened. הָאָב > הַאָּב*

   b. ה and ח, although rejecting dāḡēš forte,
nearly always imply its presence and
thus allow the preceding vowel to remain

---

*The asterisk is used to indicate original or
hypothetical forms not actually found in the
language.

short. *הַחֹּשֶׁךְ > הַחֹשֶׁךְ

2. Prefer an "a" class vowel before and sometimes after them. The pat̲aḥ furtive is an example of this tendency. Cf. §6.
3. Prefer a compound shewa instead of simple shewa. Cf. §8.1.c.

Note: א and ה normally do not close a syllable (except ה with mappîq) and are almost always preceded by a long vowel.

PART II

§14. The Article

Hebrew has no indefinite article. A word without the article usually receives in translation the English indefinite article. The definite article is always an inseparable prefix, never an independent word. The normal form of the article is ·הַ (hê paṯaḥ plus dāḡēš forte in the following consonant).

הַשָּׁמַיִם 1:1 הַמָּיִם 1:2

Before laryngeals the article has the following peculiarities:

1. Before א, ע, and ר, which reject the dāḡēš forte, the vowel of the article is usually lengthened.

   הָאוֹר 1:3 הָרָקִיעַ 1:7 הָעוֹף 1:22

2. Before ה and ח, which imply the dāḡēš forte, the normal vowel of the article remains.

   הַחֹשֶׁךְ 1:4 הַהֹלֵךְ 2:14

3. Before חָ, חֳ, or unaccented הָ, עָ, the vowel of the article is s^{e}ḡôl.

   הֶעָפָר הֶהָרִים הֶחֳלִי הֶחָג

Note: עַם people, אֶרֶץ earth, and הַר mountain, however, are vocalized with the article as follows: הָעָם הָאָרֶץ 1:1 הָהָר

§15. The Inseparable Preposition

The inseparable prepositions are:

בְּ 'in,' 'with,' 'by'

כְּ 'as,' 'like,' 'according to'

לְ 'to,' 'for,' 'at'

They are prefixed to the noun in the following manner:

1. Before consonants having a vowel the preposi-

tion bears a vocal shewa.

בְּרֵאשִׁית 1:1 בְּתוֹךְ 1:6

2. Before consonants having a vocal shewa:

a. Simple shewa:

Since a vocal shewa may not immediately precede another vocal shewa, the shewa of the preposition becomes ḥîreq.

בְּ+רְקִיעַ < בִּרְקִיעַ 1:14

לְ+מְשֹׁל < לִמְשֹׁל 1:18

When the preposition is prefixed to a word beginning with yôd bearing vocal shewa (יְ), the shewa of the preposition becomes ḥîreq in accordance with the rule. The yôd, however, now loses its consonantal value and coalesces with the ḥîreq, thus becoming long ḥîreq. It loses its shewa.

בְּ+יְהוּדָה < *בְּיְהוּדָה < *בִּיְהוּדָה < בִּיהוּדָה

b. Compound shewa:

The preposition prefixed to a consonant bearing compound shewa takes the vowel sign corresponding to that of the compound shewa and is written with a meteg.

לְ+עֲבֹד < לַֽעֲבֹד 2:5 ֲ ַֽ

בְּ+אֱמֶת < בֶּֽאֱמֶת ֱ ֶֽ

בְּ+חֳלִי < בָּֽחֳלִי ֳ ָֽ

3. Before the article:

When the preposition is prefixed to a noun with the article, the preposition loses its shewa and supplants the ה of the article, but retains the pointing of the article.

לְ+הָאוֹר < לָאוֹר 1:5

לְ+הַחֹשֶׁךְ < לַחֹשֶׁךְ 1:5

בְּ+הַיּוֹם < בַּיּוֹם 1:18

בְּ+הֶחֳלִי < בֶּחֳלִי

4. Before the accented syllable the preposition

sometimes takes qāmeṣ. .
לָמָּיִם 1:6; לָכֶם 1:29; לָדַעַת 3:22

§16. The Preposition מִן 'from,' 'out of'

The preposition מִן may be written either separably or inseparably.

1. The separable מִן normally with following maqqēp̄ appears almost exclusively before the article. מִן־הָאָרֶץ 'from the earth' 2:6
2. The inseparable מִן is prefixed to words without the article as follows:
   a. When מִן is written inseparably with the following word, the ן is assimilated to the following consonant as shown by the dāḡēš forte.
      מִן+קוֹל < *מִנְקוֹל < מִקּוֹל 'from a voice'
      מִן+תַּחַת < *מִנְתַּחַת < מִתַּחַת 'from underneath' 1:7
      (Observe that dāḡēš lēnē becomes dāḡēš forte.)

   Note: This phenomenon appears in some English words, i.e., *inlegible has become 'illegible'; *inlegitimate has become 'illegitimate.'

   b. Since the laryngeals reject dāḡēš forte:
      1) Before א, ע, ר the ḥîreq of מִן is lengthened to ṣērē to compensate for the loss of the dāḡēš forte.
         מִן+עַל < *מִנְעַל < מֵעַל 'from upon' 1:7
         מִן+אִישׁ < *מִנְאִישׁ < מֵאִישׁ 'from a man' 2:23
         מִן+רֹאשׁ < *מִנְרֹאשׁ < מֵרֹאשׁ 'from a head'
      2) Before ה and ח in which the dāḡēš forte is implied, the ḥîreq of מִן is not lengthened.
         מִן+חוּץ < *מִנְחוּץ < מִחוּץ 'from a street,' 'from outside' 6:14
         מִן+הַר < *מִנְהַר < מִהַר 'from a mountain'

c. Before a word having initial yôd with shewa (יְ), the ן of מִן assimilates to yôd. The resulting מִיְּ is contracted to מִי. Cf. §15.2.a.

מִיהוּדָה < *מִיְּהוּדָה < *מִנְיְהוּדָה < מִן+יְהוּדָה

d. In rare instances מִן is prefixed inseparably to words with the article.

מֵהָאָרֶץ 'from the earth'

§17. The Conjunction

The conjunction 'and' in Hebrew is expressed by wāw with vocal shewa (וְ) prefixed to any word. The conjunction never stands alone.

It is prefixed as follows:

1. Normally וְ

   וְאֵת 1:1 וְהָאָרֶץ 1:2

2. Before consonants with vocal shewa as well as before the labials ב, מ, פ, the conjunction וְ becomes וּ.

   וּלְמִקְוֵה 1:10 וּבֵין 1:4 וּמִלְאוּ 1:22 וּפָנִים

   Note: Before yôd with vocal shewa (יְ) the combination is written and pronounced וִי. Cf. §15.2.a.

   וִיהִי < *וְיְהִי < וְ+יְהִי 1:6

3. Before compound shewa the wāw receives the vowel sign corresponding to the compound shewa and is written with a meteg. Cf. §15.2.b.

   וַאֲנִי 6:17 וֶאֱמֶת וַחֲלִי

4. Immediately before the accented syllable the wāw often takes ָ. Cf. §15.4.

   וָבֹהוּ 1:2

Note: The prefixed וַ· as in וַיֹּאמֶר 1:3 will be considered later.

§18. Independent Personal Pronouns

1. The independent personal pronoun is inflected as follows:

		Singular	in pause		Plural	in pause
1c.	I	אֲנִי אָנֹכִי	אָֽנִי אָנֹֽכִי	we	אֲנַחְנוּ (נַחְנוּ)	אֲנָֽחְנוּ (נָֽחְנוּ)
2m.	you	אַתָּה	אָֽתָּה אַֽתָּה	you	אַתֶּם	
2f.	you	אַתְּ	אָֽתְּ	you	אַתֵּ֫נָה (אַתֵּן, אַתֶּן)	
3m.	he	הוּא		they	הֵם, הֵֽמָּה	
3f.	she	הִיא		they	הֵן, הֵֽנָּה	

Note 1: Pausal forms are listed for the sake of completeness.

Note 2: The forms in parentheses occur less frequently.

Note 3: The abbreviation c. means common gender.

Note 4: The accent of a word in pause often shifts from the ultima to the penult. Observe the vowel change. Cf. §12.3.

2. The independent pronoun is used as the subject of a sentence or a predicate nominative. These forms may combine with wāw conjunctive.

3. The pronoun in the genitive or accusative ap- pears as a shortened form, **always** affixed to a word. These suffixes will be introduced later.

§19. The Verb

Common to Semitic languages is the triliteral character of the verb; i.e., the verb in its sim- plest form normally consists of three consonants (radicals) called the root.* Preformatives and af-

---

*Quadriliteral verbs are rare. Cf. Gesenius- Kautzsch,   §56.

formatives are added to the basic root to indicate number, person, and gender as well as changes of meaning and condition of the action.

The Hebrew verbal system is altogether different from the verbal system of the Indo-European languages with which one is familiar. The Hebrew verb describes the action as complete or incomplete, whereas the verb in Indo-European languages is temporal in character. In Hebrew, tense must be derived from the context. Following the terminology of most grammarians this text has adopted the terms 'perfect' to describe completed action, and 'imperfect' to describe incomplete action. The student must remember that perfect and imperfect indicate not time but state of action.

The basic form of the verb is the third masculine singular (3ms) Qal. This is equivalent to the root and is the form found in the lexicon. The term 'Qal' (קַל) means "light." It is the term used to describe the simplest conjugation of the verb. Other conjugations "are weighted" by the addition of at least one consonant to the verb.

A verb root consisting of three radicals, none of which is either a laryngeal or a vowel letter, is called a strong verb.

THE STUDENT MUST MASTER THE STRONG VERB IN ITS ENTIRETY.

§20. Afformatives to the Perfect

The pronominal afformatives to the perfect are:

Singular			Plural		
3m.	--	he	3c.	וּ	they
3f.	ָה	she			
2m.	תָּ	you	2m.	תֶּם	you
2f.	תְּ	you	2f.	תֶּן	you
1c.	תִּי	I	1c.	נוּ	we

These afformatives are classified:

1. Vocalic (ָה and וּ) because they begin with a vowel; they normally draw the accent.
2. Consonantal when they begin with a consonant.
   a. Light consonantal: תָ, תְ, תִי, נוּ; these do not normally draw the accent.
   b. Heavy consonantal: תֶם, תֶן; these always draw the accent.

The perfect never adds pronominal preformatives.

§21. *Vowel Changes Within Syllables*

Since the addition of preformatives and/or afformatives may cause syllabic or accentual change within the word, the vowels of the word may also undergo change.

1. The length of the vowels in *unaccented* syllables will *normally* be determined according to the following rules:
   a. A closed unaccented syllable requires a short vowel.
   Note: Before dāgēš forte the vowel of the closed syllable will be pataḥ, ḥîreq, or qibbûṣ rather than segôl or qāmeṣ ḥāṭûp.
   b. An open unaccented syllable normally requires a long vowel; or, in a verb, it may take vocal shewa.
   c. The vowel in a distant open syllable (at least two syllables from the accent) reduces to vocal shewa, unless followed by vocal shewa, in which case it takes a meteg.

The following table will help to illustrate the above rules:

Kind of syllable (unaccented)	Class of vowel a	i	u	
Closed	◌ַ or ◌ֶ	◌ִ or ◌ֶ	◌ֻ or ◌ָ	Short vowel
Near open	◌ָ	◌ֵ	◌ֹ	Lengthened vowel
Distant open	◌ְ or ◌ֲ	◌ְ or ◌ֱ	◌ְ or ◌ֳ	Reduced vowel

Note: A near open syllable is an open syllable immediately preceding an accented syllable.

2. Accented syllables:

The vowel of an accented syllable may be long or short, the syllable open or closed.

Note 1: The vocal shewa never bears an accent, nor can it stand in a closed syllable.

Note 2: Short vowels, if lengthened, are normally lengthened to the corresponding long vowel, e.g., paṯaḥ to qāmeṣ, ḥîreq to ṣērē, qibbûṣ to ḥōlem.

§22. <u>Conjugation of the Perfect Qal of the Verb קטל, 'to kill'</u>

(Note: The root, in itself an abstraction, may be conveniently translated by the English infinitive. Thus קטל, 'to kill,' but קָטַל, 'he killed.')

1. 3 m. s. קָטַל, 'he killed.' The third masculine singular Qal perfect usually has qāmeṣ under the first radical, paṯaḥ under the second.

Note 1: If the word bears no written accent, the tone falls on the ultima (Cf. §11.1).

Note 2: Most intransitive verbs (called statives) and a few transitives have as the second vowel a ṣērē, occasionally a ḥōlem, e.g., כָּבֵד, קָטֹן. Cf. paradigm, p. 105.

2. 3 f.s. קָטְלָה, 'she killed.'

a. Since the afformative ָה begins with a vowel and thus cannot begin a syllable (Cf. §7), it takes the ל of קָטַל to form a syllable לָה, leaving *קָטְ. <u>The vocalic afformative draws the accent</u>.

b. In the penult, as normally before vocalic afformatives, the vowel reduces to vocal shewa instead of being lengthened. Cf. §21.1.b. This vowel never becomes silent shewa. This form in pause becomes קָטָ֫לָה.

c. In the antepenult the long vowel before vocal shewa requires a me<u>t</u>e<u>g</u>. Cf. §11.2.Note.

3. 2 m.s. קָטַ֫לְתָּ, 'you (m.) killed.'

a. תָּ is a light consonantal afformative and does not draw the accent. (An exception with wāw consecutive will be explained later.)

b. Since תָּ is itself a syllable and does not draw the accent it is simply affixed to the 3 m.s. form קָטַל. The silent shewa is necessary since ל now closes a syllable <u>within</u> the word. Since the <u>penult</u> is accented, the accent is written (Cf. §11.1).

4. 2 f.s. קָטַלְתְּ, 'you (f.) killed.'

a. Normally two silent shewas do not occur together.

b. The afformative תְּ represents an exception to the above rule. The afformative was originally תִּי; the ḥîreq yô<u>d</u>, however, has dropped out in the leveling process of the language (it recurs before pronominal suffixes), leaving תְּ with a silent shewa (תְ).

Note: טַלְתְּ is called a doubly closed syllable because it ends with two consonants.

5. 1 c.s. קָטַלְתִּי, 'I killed.'
The afformative תִּי is affixed to the 3 m.s. form on the analogy of 3 above.

6. 3 c.p. קָטְלוּ, 'they killed.'
The afformative וּ is affixed to the 3 m.s. form קָטַל with vocalic changes as in 2 above.

7. 2 m.p. קְטַלְתֶּם, 'you (m.p.) killed.'
a. תֶּם is a heavy consonantal afformative and always draws the accent.
b. The טַל of קָטַל is a closed unaccented syllable and remains unchanged.
c. Since the syllable קָ of קָטַל is now distant open, the qāmeṣ reduces to vocal shewa (see vowel table, §21).

8. 2 f.p. קְטַלְתֶּן, 'you (f.p.) killed.'
The afformative תֶּן is affixed to the stem קָטַל on the analogy of 7 above.

9. 1 c.p. קָטַלְנוּ, 'we killed.'
The afformative נוּ is affixed to the stem קָטַל on the analogy of 3 above.

The conjugation of the perfect Qal appears thus:

Singular			Plural		
3 m.	קָטַל	he killed	3 c.	קָטְלוּ	they killed
3 f.	קָטְלָה	she "			
2 m.	קָטַלְתָּ	you "	2 m.	קְטַלְתֶּם	you "
2 f.	קָטַלְתְּ	you "	2 f.	קְטַלְתֶּן	you "
1 c.	קָטַלְתִּי	I "	1 c.	קָטַלְנוּ	we "

§23. Conjugation of the Imperfect Qal of the Verb קָטַל

The imperfect is distinguished by always having a pronominal preformative. Some inflections also add an afformative.

The pronominal preformatives and afformatives are:

Singular			Plural		
3 m.	___י	he	3 m.	וּ___י	they
3 f.	___ת	she	3 f.	נָה___ת	they
2 m.	___ת	you	2 m.	וּ___ת	you
2 f.	ִי___ת	you	2 f.	נָה___ת	you
1 c.	___א	I	1 c.	___נ	we

Note: For classification of afformatives see §20.1, 2. נָה is a light consonantal afformative.

1. 3 m.s. יִקְטֹל 'he will kill.'

   a. The preformative of the imperfect Qal forms with the first radical of the root a closed syllable.

      Note: The hîreq following the י was originally a paṯaḥ and has been attenuated (thinned).

   b. The thematic vowel of the imperfect Qal (the ultima vowel of the 3 m.s. imperfect) in the strong verb is usually lengthened ḥōlem (from an original qibbûṣ).

      The thematic vowel of the imperfect Qal may be of the "a," "i," or "u" class.

      Note: The vowels of the 3 m.s. Qal imperfect will serve as a pattern for the inflection of the entire Qal imperfect.

2. 3 f.s. תִּקְטֹל 'she will kill'

3. 2 m.s. תִּקְטֹל 'you will kill'

4. 2 f.s. תִּקְטְלִי 'you will kill'
Since the vocalic afformative draws the accent, the previous ḥōlem reduces to vocal shewa. Cf. §22.2.b.
Note: Two shewas together. Cf. §8.note 1.

5. 1 c.s. אֶקְטֹל 'I will kill'
The s^{e}g̱ôl is probably to be explained by the fact that the א has a preference for this sound.

6. 3 m.p. יִקְטְלוּ 'they will kill'
Cf. 4 above.

7. 3 f.p. תִּקְטֹלְנָה 'they will kill'
Since נָה is a light consonantal afformative, the ḥōlem remains with the accent.

8. 2 m.p. תִּקְטְלוּ 'you will kill'
Cf. 4 above.

9. 2 f.p. תִּקְטֹלְנָה 'you will kill'
Cf. 7 above.

10. 1 c.p. נִקְטֹל 'we will kill'

The conjugation of the Qal imperfect appears thus:

Singular		Plural	
3m.	יִקְטֹל he will kill	3m.	יִקְטְלוּ they will kill
3f.	תִּקְטֹל she will kill	3f.	תִּקְטֹלְנָה they will kill
2m.	תִּקְטֹל you will kill	2m.	תִּקְטְלוּ you will kill
2f.	תִּקְטְלִי you will kill	2f.	תִּקְטֹלְנָה you will kill
1c.	אֶקְטֹל I will kill	1c.	נִקְטֹל we will kill

Note: The shewa before a vocalic afformative of a verb <u>in pause</u> reverts to its original vowel and takes the accent. If the vowel was short, it is normally lengthened. Cf. §18.1, note 4.

יִקְטְלוּ < יִקְטֹ֫לוּ

יִתְבֹּשְׁשׁוּ < יִתְבֹּשָׁ֫שׁוּ 2:25

קָטְלָה < קָטָ֫לָה

נִפְתְּחוּ < נִפְתָּ֫חוּ 7:11

§24. <u>The Conjugation of the Imperative Qal</u>

The imperative is formed exactly as the imperfect with the omission of the pronominal preformative.

1. 2 m.s. קְטֹל 'kill'

   Note: The silent shewa of the imperfect now becomes vocal. Cf. §8.note 2.

2. 2 f.s. קִטְלִי 'kill'

   Note: When the preformative of the imperfect is dropped, the silent shewa becomes vocal, i.e., *קְטְלִי. Since two vocal shewas may not stand together, the first becomes ḥîreq. Cf. §15.2.a., also §8.note 5.

3. 2 m.p. קִטְלוּ 'kill'

   Cf. 2 above.

4. 2 f.p. קְטֹלְנָה 'kill'

   Cf. 1 above.

The conjugation of the Qal imperative appears thus:

Singular			Plural		
2 m.	קְטֹל	kill	2 m.	קִטְלוּ	kill
2 f.	קִטְלִי	kill	2 f.	קְטֹלְנָה	kill

§25. Qal Infinitives and Participles

1. The infinitives are nouns (verbal substantives).
   a. The infinitive absolute is קָטוֹל, 'killing.' This infinitive normally serves to strengthen the verb, e.g., Deut. 7:18 "remembering you shall remember," i.e., "you shall surely remember." זָכוֹר תִּזְכֹּר
      Note: The vowels of this form are unchangeable.
   b. The infinitive construct is קְטֹל, 'to kill,' 'killing.' This is a shortened form of the infinitive absolute.
      Note 1: The vowels of this form are changeable.
      Note 2: The form is identical with the imperative 2 m.s.
2. The participles, while nouns in form, may be considered verbal adjectives; they are timeless, i.e., they may refer to present, future, or past time.
   a. The active participle is קֹטֵל, 'killing.'
   b. The passive participle is קָטוּל, 'killed.' This form is a vestige of an original Qal passive conjugation.

§26. Stative Verbs

Verbs which express a state or condition of being are called 'statives,' e.g., יָרֵא, 'he was afraid'; קָטֹן, 'he was small.' These are distinguished by the vowel under the second radical only in certain forms of the Qal. Refer to paradigms.

1. With ṣērē in the 3 m.s. perfect, e.g., כָּבֵד, 'he was heavy.' The remaining forms of the perfect take paṯaḥ, as in the strong verb. The thematic vowel of the imperfect and imperative is paṯaḥ. The active participle is the same as the 3 m.s. perfect in form.
2. With ḥōlem in 3 m.s. perfect, e.g., קָטֹן. This

ḥōlem remains throughout the perfect where pa-ṯaḥ normally would occur, except before the afformatives תֶּם and תֶּן where it bears qāmeṣ ḥāṭûp̱. The thematic vowel in imperfect and imperative is paṯaḥ. The active participle is the same as the 3 m.s. perfect in form.

3. With paṯaḥ in the 3 m.s. perfect, e.g., קָדַשׁ, 'he was holy.' These verbs are not distinguishable in form from the regular verb.

§27. The Remaining Conjugations

In addition to the Qal there are six so-called "conjugations" of the verb.

The conjugations are:

1.	Qal	קַל	Root meaning
2.	Nip̱ʿal	נִפְעַל	Reflexive, sometimes passive
3.	Piʿēl	פִּעֵל	Intensive active
4.	Puʿal	פֻּעַל	Intensive passive
5.	Hiṯpaʿēl	הִתְפַּעֵל	Intensive reflexive
6.	Hip̱ʿîl	הִפְעִיל	Causative active
7.	Hop̱ʿal	הָפְעַל	Causative passive

Note 1: The student will observe that the derived stems are based on a root פעל. This root is used as a mnemonic device, borrowed from Arab grammarians, to describe the conjugations.

Note 2: Only a few verbs appear in all seven conjugations. Verbs which occur only in Piʿēl, Puʿal, or Hiṯpaʿēl are thereby not necessarily intensive in meaning; verbs which occur only in Hip̱ʿîl or Hop̱ʿal are thereby not necessarily causative in meaning.

§28. The Nip̱ʿal

1. The primary characteristic of the Nip̱ʿal in all its forms is a prefixed נ.

2. The prefix נִ of the perfect and participle (attenuated from original נַ) is prefixed to the simple stem to form with the first radical a closed syllable.

   a. The perfect afformatives are identical throughout the conjugations. Thus:

	Singular			Plural
3 m.	נִקְטַל	'he killed himself,' 'he was killed'	3 c.	נִקְטְלוּ
3 f.	נִקְטְלָה			
2 m.	נִקְטַלְתָּ		2 m.	נִקְטַלְתֶּם
2 f.	נִקְטַלְתְּ		2 f.	נִקְטַלְתֶּן
1 c.	נִקְטַלְתִּי		1 c.	נִקְטַלְנוּ

   b. The participle is נִקְטָל, 'killed.' Note the distinction between 3 m.s. perfect and participle forms.

3. The distinguishing characteristic of the Nip̱ʿal imperfect is the assimilated נ:

	Singular		Plural
3 m.	יִקָּטֵל	3 m.	יִקָּטְלוּ
3 f.	תִּקָּטֵל	3 f.	תִּקָּטַלְנָה
2 m.	תִּקָּטֵל	2 m.	תִּקָּטְלוּ
2 f.	תִּקָּטְלִי	2 f.	תִּקָּטַלְנָה
1 c.	אֶקָּטֵל	1 c.	נִקָּטֵל

   Note: Before the afformative נָה the vowel is usually paṯaḥ, sometimes ṣērē.

4. The Nip̱ʿal imperative and infinitives have the prefix הִנְ, the נ of which is assimilated to the following letter.

   a. The imperative:

2 m.s.	הִקָּטֵל	2 m.p.	הִקָּטְלוּ
2 f.s.	הִקָּטְלִי	2 f.p.	הִקָּטַלְנָה

   b. The infinitives:

   Absolute הִקָּטֹל (נִקְטֹל)

   Construct הִקָּטֵל

§29. <u>The Intensives</u>: <u>Piʿēl</u>, <u>Puʿal</u>, <u>Hitpaʿēl</u>

The intensives are characterized by the doubling of the middle radical of the stem.

1. <u>Piʿēl</u>

Piʿēl perfect

Singular			Plural	
3 m.	קִטֵּל	'he killed (with brutality)'	3 c.	קִטְּלוּ
3 f.	קִטְּלָה			
2 m.	קִטַּלְתָּ		2 m.	קִטַּלְתֶּם
2 f.	קִטַּלְתְּ		2 f.	קִטַּלְתֶּן
1 c.	קִטַּלְתִּי		1 c.	קִטַּלְנוּ

Note: Observe the paṯaḥ in the penult before consonantal afformatives.

Piʿēl imperfect

3 m.	יְקַטֵּל	3 m.	יְקַטְּלוּ
3 f.	תְּקַטֵּל	3 f.	תְּקַטֵּלְנָה
2 m.	תְּקַטֵּל	2 m.	תְּקַטְּלוּ
2 f.	תְּקַטְּלִי	2 f.	תְּקַטֵּלְנָה
1 c.	אֲקַטֵּל	1 c.	נְקַטֵּל

Note: Observe ṣērē before consonantal נָה. It may sometimes be paṯaḥ.

Piʿēl imperative

2 m.	קַטֵּל	2 m.	קַטְּלוּ
2 f.	קַטְּלִי	2 f.	קַטֵּלְנָה

Piʿēl infinitives

Absolute קַטֹּל

Construct קַטֵּל

Piʿēl participle

מְקַטֵּל

Note: All participles except Qal and Nipʿal have a prefixed מ.

2. <u>Puʿal</u>

Puʿal perfect

	Singular			Plural
3 m.	קֻטַּל	'he was killed (with brutality)'	3 c.	קֻטְּלוּ
3 f.	קֻטְּלָה			
2 m.	קֻטַּלְתָּ		2 m.	קֻטַּלְתֶּם
2 f.	קֻטַּלְתְּ		2 f.	קֻטַּלְתֶּן
1 c.	קֻטַּלְתִּי		1 c.	קֻטַּלְנוּ

Puʿal imperfect

3 m.	יְקֻטַּל	3 m.	יְקֻטְּלוּ
3 f.	תְּקֻטַּל	3 f.	תְּקֻטַּלְנָה
2 m.	תְּקֻטַּל	2 m.	תְּקֻטְּלוּ
2 f.	תְּקֻטְּלִי	2 f.	תְּקֻטַּלְנָה
1 c.	אֲקֻטַּל	1 c.	נְקֻטַּל

Puʿal imperative

(none) (none)

Puʿal infinitives

Absolute קֻטֹּל

Construct קֻטַּל

Puʿal participle

מְקֻטָּל

Note: The characteristic vowel of Puʿal is qibbûṣ.

3. <u>Hiṯpaʿēl</u>

The primary characteristic of the Hiṯpaʿēl is the prefixed הִתְ.

Hiṯpaʿēl perfect

	Singular			Plural
3 m.	הִתְקַטֵּל	'he killed himself'	3 c.	הִתְקַטְּלוּ
3 f.	הִתְקַטְּלָה			
2 m.	הִתְקַטַּלְתָּ		2 m.	הִתְקַטַּלְתֶּם
2 f.	הִתְקַטַּלְתְּ		2 f.	הִתְקַטַּלְתֶּן
1 c.	הִתְקַטַּלְתִּי		1 c.	הִתְקַטַּלְנוּ

Note the paṯaḥ in the penult before consonantal afformatives.

Hit̲paʿēl imperfect

Singular		Plural	
3 m.	יִתְקַטֵּל	3 m.	יִתְקַטְּלוּ
3 f.	תִּתְקַטֵּל	3 f.	תִּתְקַטֵּלְנָה
2 m.	תִּתְקַטֵּל	2 m.	תִּתְקַטְּלוּ
2 f.	תִּתְקַטְּלִי	2 f.	תִּתְקַטֵּלְנָה
1 c.	אֶתְקַטֵּל	1 c.	נִתְקַטֵּל

Hit̲paʿēl imperative

2 m.	הִתְקַטֵּל	2 m.	הִתְקַטְּלוּ
2 f.	הִתְקַטְּלִי	2 f.	הִתְקַטֵּלְנָה

Hit̲paʿēl infinitives

Absolute הִתְקַטֹּל

Construct הִתְקַטֵּל

Hit̲paʿēl participle

מִתְקַטֵּל

Note 1: If the verb begins with one of the sibilants שׂ שׁ צ ס the position of the sibilant and the ת of the preformative (הִתְ) is transposed (metathesis), e.g., הִשְׁתַּמֵּר < *הִתְשַׁמֵּר.

Note 2: If the sibilant is צ, the ת in addition to being transposed becomes ט, e.g., *הִתְצַדֵּק > הִצְטַדֵּק.

Note 3: The ת of the preformative is assimilated to following ד, ט, or ת, e.g., הִטַּהֵר.

§30. <u>The Causatives: Hip̲ʿîl and Hop̲ʿal</u>

The characteristic of the causatives is the prefixed ה.

1. <u>The Hip̲ʿîl</u>.

Hip̲ʿîl perfect

The preformative of the Hip̲ʿîl perfect is הַ attenuated to הִ which forms with the first radical of the stem a closed syllable.

Singular			Plural	
3 m.	הִקְטִיל	'he caused to kill'	3 c.	הִקְטִ֫ילוּ
3 f.	הִקְטִ֫ילָה			
2 m.	הִקְטַ֫לְתָּ		2 m.	הִקְטַלְתֶּם
2 f.	הִקְטַלְתְּ		2 f.	הִקְטַלְתֶּן
1 c.	הִקְטַ֫לְתִּי		1 c.	הִקְטַ֫לְנוּ

Note 1: Before vocalic afformatives the ִי is retained with the accent.

Note 2: The vowels ִי and וּ may not stand in a closed syllable unless it be the ultima. Therefore, before consonantal afformatives, the ִי of the Hip̱ʿîl reverts to an original pataḥ.

Hip̱ʿîl imperfect

The characteristic of the imperfect is the preformative ַ from original יְהַ.

3 m.	יַקְטִיל	3 m.	יַקְטִ֫ילוּ
3 f.	תַּקְטִיל	3 f.	תַּקְטֵ֫לְנָה
2 m.	תַּקְטִיל	2 m.	תַּקְטִ֫ילוּ
2 f.	תַּקְטִ֫ילִי	2 f.	תַּקְטֵ֫לְנָה
1 c.	אַקְטִיל	1 c.	נַקְטִיל

Note: Observe the ṣērē before the afformative נָה. Since ִי may not stand in a closed syllable followed by a consonant (Cf. note 2 above), the ִי becomes ֵ .

Hip̱ʿîl imperative

2 m.	הַקְטֵל	2 m.	הַקְטִ֫ילוּ
2 f.	הַקְטִ֫ילִי	2 f.	הַקְטֵ֫לְנָה

Note 1: Observe ṣērē in the ultima of 2 m.s.

Note 2: Observe הַ as distinguished from הִ of the perfect prefix.

Hip̱ʿîl infinitives

Absolute הַקְטֵל

Construct הַקְטִיל

Hip̱ʿîl participle

מַקְטִיל

2. The Hop̱ʿal.

Hop̱ʿal perfect

Singular			Plural	
3 m.	הָקְטַל	'he was caused to kill'	3 c.	הָקְטְלוּ
3 f.	הָקְטְלָה			
2 m.	הָקְטַלְתָּ		2 m.	הָקְטַלְתֶּם
2 f.	הָקְטַלְתְּ		2 f.	הָקְטַלְתֶּן
1 c.	הָקְטַלְתִּי		1 c.	הָקְטַלְנוּ

Hop̱ʿal imperfect

3 m.	יָקְטַל	3 m.	יָקְטְלוּ
3 f.	תָּקְטַל	3 f.	תָּקְטַלְנָה
2 m.	תָּקְטַל	2 m.	תָּקְטְלוּ
2 f.	תָּקְטְלִי	2 f.	תָּקְטַלְנָה
1 c.	אָקְטַל	1 c.	נָקְטַל

Hop̱ʿal imperative

(none)

Hop̱ʿal infinitives

Absolute הָקְטֵל

Construct הָקְטַל

Hop̱ʿal participle

מָקְטָל

Note: Observe that all passive participles have qāmeṣ in the ultima.

> The student must acquire a thorough mastery of the strong verb in order to understand the irregular verbs. This necessity cannot be too strongly emphasized.

§31. The Jussive and Cohortative

The jussive is a shortened form of the imperfect and the cohortative is a lengthened one.

1. The Jussive.

a. The jussive is usually formed from the second or third person, singular and plural, to express a wish or a command.

b. In the strong verb the jussive is not distinguished in form from the imperfect indicative except in the Hip̱ʿîl.

1. The context determines whether the form is jussive or the regular imperfect indicative.

2. In the Hip̱ʿîl <u>without</u> afformative or suffix the jussive is formed by changing ḥîreq yô<u>d</u> to ṣērē (ִי to ֵ). תַּדְשֵׁא 1:11. <u>With</u> a suffix or afformative the ḥîreq yô<u>d</u> remains.

תַּקְטִיל < תַּקְטֵל ,

but תַּקְטִֽילִי remains תַּקְטִֽילִי

c. The jussive tends to cause the accent to move to an open penult when the ultima is a closed syllable.

Note: The jussive as a regularly shortened form of the imperfect occurs only in certain weak verbs.

2. The Cohortative.

a. The cohortative, the lengthened form of the imperfect, is usually formed from the first person singular or plural to express self-encouragement or a wish.

b. This form is distinguished by the addition of ָה which usually draws the accent.

אֶקְטְלָה 'Let me kill' or 'Oh, that I may kill'

נִשְׂרְפָה , נִלְבְּנָה 11:3 אֲגַדְּלָה 12:2

A changeable vowel before the ending ָה is reduced to shewa. An unchangeable vowel retains the accent.

In pause, the vowel which would normally be reduced to shewa is retained with the accent. נִקְטְלָה נִקְטֹֽלָה

c. The cohortative ending is often added to

the 2 m.s. of the imperative, generally for the sake of emphasis.
קָטְלָה < קְטֹל qoṭlâ Cf. §8.note 5.
הַקְטִ֫ילָה < הַקְטֵל

§32. <u>The</u> <u>Wāw</u> <u>Consecutive</u> (<u>Conversive</u>)

A stylistic device of narrative Ḥebrew is the wāw consecutive, used to narrate consecutive events in past or future time (hence the name 'consecutive').

1. With the imperfect:
   a. This wāw is prefixed to the imperfect with paṯaḥ and following dāḡēš forte. The pointing is identical with that of the article, e.g., וַיֹּ֫אמֶר 1:3; וָאֹכֵל 3:13.
   Note: Observe that doubled consonants when they bear a vocal shewa may drop the dāḡēš forte. This occurs most frequently with יְ after wāw consecutive. Other consonants which with vocal shewa often drop the dāḡēš forte are ו, ל, מ, נ, ק, and the sibilants שׂ, שׁ, ז, ס, צ; e.g., וַיְהִי 1:3.
   b. The wāw consecutive tends to draw the accent to an open penult. In the strong verb this occurs only in the Nip̄ʿal. When this occurs the long vowel of the ultima may be reduced. וַיִּקָּ֫טֶל < יִקָּטֵל
   c. In the Hip̄ʿîl ḥîreq yôḏ becomes ṣērē after wāw consecutive except in the 1 c.s.
   וַיַּבְדֵּל < יַבְדִּיל 1:4 וָאַקְטִיל < אַקְטִיל
   Note: When pronominal suffixes are added, the ḥîreq yôḏ is maintained.
2. With the perfect:
   a. The wāw consecutive is prefixed to the perfect exactly as the wāw conjunctive.

Normally the context must determine whether the wāw is consecutive or conjunctive.

b. The accent usually moves from the penult to the ultima in 2 m.s. or 1 c.s. forms.
וְקָטַלְתִּי < קָטַלְתִּי   וְקָטַלְתָּ < קָטַלְתָּ

3. The use of the wāw consecutive:

a. Narration of past events begins in the perfect and continues in the imperfect introduced by wāw consecutive. The imperfect with wāw consecutive is therefore translated as a perfect, e.g., "In the beginning God created (בָּרָא) . . . and the earth was (הָיְתָה) . . . and God said (וַיֹּאמֶר) . . ." 1:1-3.

If in continued narration the wāw is separated from its verb (imperfect), the verb form reverts from imperfect to perfect, e.g., "And God called (וַיִּקְרָא) . . . and the darkness He called (קָרָא) . . ." 1:5.

b. Narration of present or future events begins in the imperfect and continues in the perfect with wāw consecutive. The perfect with wāw consecutive is therefore translated as an imperfect, e.g., "And God said, 'Let there be (יְהִי) . . . and let them be (וְהָיוּ) . . .'" 1:14. If the wāw is separated from its verb (perfect), the verb form reverts from the perfect to the imperfect, e.g., "When the Egyptians shall see thee, they shall say (וְאָמְרוּ), 'This is his wife': and they will kill me (וְהָרְגוּ אֹתִי) but thee will they save alive (וְאֹתָךְ יְחַיּוּ)" 12:12.

Note: The wāw consecutive, like the jussive, tends to cause the accent to move to an open penult. If, however, the ultima is an open syllable, it retains the accent even though the penult be an open syllable.

§33. The Noun

1. Nouns in Hebrew are masculine or feminine; singular, plural, or dual. The neuter does not exist.

   Case endings are extremely rare. The so-called "cases" (nominative, genitive, accusative), therefore, must be inferred from the context. חַיְתוֹ 1:24 (ḥōlem wāw is an old case ending). The accusative is often indicated by the particle אֵת. אֵת הַשָּׁמַיִם 1:1
2. The masculine singular noun has no distinguishing ending. Normally the feminine singular noun ends with ־ָה (original ־ַת).
3. The masculine plural noun normally ends with ־ִים. The feminine plural noun normally ends with ־וֹת.
4. The dual ending for both masculine and feminine is ־ַיִם.

	Masculine	Feminine
Singular	סוּס horse	סוּסָה mare
Plural	סוּסִים horses	סוּסוֹת mares
Dual	סוּסַיִם two horses	סוּסָתַיִם two mares

Observe that the affix draws the accent.

Note 1: The feminine noun is not always distinguished by the affix ־ָה. Some nouns are feminine by nature.

אֶרֶץ 'earth' 1:1 נֶפֶשׁ 'soul' 1:20
רוּחַ 'spirit' 1:2 אֵם 'mother' 2:24

Note 2: The endings ִית, וּת, ֶת are feminine.

רֵאשִׁית 1:1 מְרַחֶפֶת 1:2

Note 3: The affixes to nouns ָה, ִים, וֹת, since they draw the accent, may cause the vowels of the noun to undergo change.

singular מוֹעֵד plural מוֹעֲדִים 1:14

Note 4: Some masculine nouns take a feminine plural ending and some feminine nouns take a masculine plural ending.

Singular		Plural	
שָׁנָה	'year'	שָׁנִים	'years' 1:14
אָב	'father'	אָבוֹת	'fathers'
מָאוֹר	'light'	מְאֹרֹת	'lights' 1:16 Cf. §4, note 1, def. writ.

§34. <u>The Construct Relation</u>

The Hebrew noun has two states: the absolute and the construct. The noun in the construct state is (when possible) a shortened form of the noun in the absolute state. The noun in the construct state must always be followed by a word in the absolute state or by a series of constructs; the construct <u>never</u> stands independently. This construct-absolute relationship corresponds in Latin to a noun modified by a genitive, e.g., 'dominus terrae.' This phenomenon is best illustrated by the relation which exists between two English words joined by 'of,' e.g., 'the Word of God' (God's Word). In Hebrew the substantive preceding an understood 'of' is called the governing noun. The governed noun is said to be in the absolute state; the governing noun, in the construct state.

Examples:

1. דְּבַר יְהוָה 'the Word of Yahweh' (a proper noun is always definite)
2. דְּבַר אִישׁ 'a word of a man'
3. סוּס הָאִישׁ 'the horse of the man'

1. Rules governing the construct relation:
   a. The construct with its dependent noun in the absolute forms one accentual unit, i.e., the primary accent falls on the absolute. The absolute always follows the construct.
   b. Since the construct loses its primary accent, its vowels (if changeable) will reduce as far as possible according to the vowel table, §21.
      Abs. דָּבָר>Const. דְּבַר in 'דְּבַר יְהוָה.'
      Abs. סוּס>Const. סוּס in 'סוּס הָאִישׁ.' The vowel of סוּס, being originally long, is unchangeable.
   c. The construct (governing noun) never takes the article. Whether or not it is definite is determined by the following absolute, which may be either definite or indefinite. Cf. examples 2 and 3 above. The absolute and construct always agree in definiteness or indefiniteness.
   d. No word ever stands between the construct and the dependent absolute.

Note: The noun is always listed in the dictionary in its singular absolute form.

2. Formation of the construct:
   a. Masculine singular construct

Abs. סוּס	'horse'	Const. סוּס	'horse (of)
דָּבָר	'word'	דְּבַר	'word (of)'
בֵּן	'son'	בֶּן	'son (of)'

   Note: There is no ending for the m.s. construct.

   b. Masculine plural construct

Abs. סוּסִים	'horses'	Const. סוּסֵי	'horses (of)'
דְּבָרִים	'words'	דִּבְרֵי	'words (of)'

   Note: The m.p. ending ִים always becomes

ֵי in construct.

Notes on vowel changes:

1. דְּבָרִים < דָּבָר according to the vowel table. The final syllable of the plural masculine construct is always considered a near open syllable. Thus in דִּבְרֵי the vowel of the original syllable בָ, which is now distant open, is reduced to shewa. The original syllable דָּ is also distant open and its vowel must be reduced to shewa; since, however, two vocal shewas cannot stand together, the first becomes ḥîreq. Cf. §15.2.a.

2. The vocalization of the m.s. participles of the strong verb is the same for absolute and construct. There is no difference in form except before suffixes.

c. Feminine singular construct

Abs. סוּסָה 'mare' Const. סוּסַת 'mare (of)'

The ending ָה always becomes ַת in construct.

d. Feminine plural construct

Abs. סוּסוֹת 'mares' Const. סוּסוֹת 'mares (of)'

The ending וֹת is unchangeable.

e. Masculine dual construct

Abs. סוּסַיִם Const. סוּסֵי

f. Feminine dual construct

Abs. סוּסָתַיִם Const. סוּסְתֵי

The dual ending ַיִם is appended to the old feminine ending ַת .

Thus:

	Absolute	Construct
m.s. m.p.	סוּס סוּסִים	סוּס סוּסֵי
f.s. f.p.	סוּסָה סוּסוֹת	סוּסַת סוּסוֹת
m. dual f. dual	סוּסַיִם סוּסָתַיִם	סוּסֵי סֻוּסְתֵי

Note: The dual is used normally only for parts of the body which appear in pairs, e.g., eyes, hands, etc.

§35. Pronominal Suffixes

The independent personal pronouns appear in the nominative case. When, however, the pronoun is dependent, i.e., in another case, it is suffixed to its governing word (noun, verb, or particle) as a shortened form of the independent pronoun.

The suffixed forms are:

Singular			Plural		
1 c.	נִי ִי	me my	1 c.	נוּ	us, our
2 m.	ךָ	you, your (sometimes כָה)	2 m.	כֶם	you, your
2 f.	ךְ	you, your	2 f.	כֶן	you, your
3 m.	הוּ, וֹ, הֹ	him, his	3 m.	הֶם, ם	them, their
3 f.	הָ, ־הּ	her, hers	3 f.	הֶן, ן	them, their

§36. Pronominal Suffixes Attached to Nouns

The suffix is always attached to the construct form of the noun. The suffix is always definite and therefore the noun to which it is affixed must also be definite.

1. To the masculine noun סוּס:

	Singular noun horse	Plural noun horses
Absolute	סוּס	סוּסִים
Construct ('of')	סוּס	סוּסֵי
1 c.s. suffix my	סוּסִי	סוּסַי
2 m.s. " your	סֽוּסְךָ	סוּסֶיךָ
2 f.s. " your	סוּסֵךְ	סוּסַיִךְ
3 m.s. " his	סוּסוֹ	סוּסָיו
3 f.s. " her	סוּסָהּ	סוּסֶיהָ
1 c.p. suffix our	סוּסֵנוּ	סוּסֵינוּ
2 m.p. " your	סֽוּסְכֶם	סֽוּסֵיכֶם
2 f.p. " your	סֽוּסְכֶן	סֽוּסֵיכֶן
3 m.p. " their	סוּסָם	סֽוּסֵיהֶם
3 f.p. " their	סוּסָן	סֽוּסֵיהֶן

2. To the feminine noun סוּסָה:

	Singular noun mare	Plural noun mares
Absolute	סוּסָה	סוּסוֹת
Construct ('of')	סוּסַת	סוּסוֹת
1 c.s. suffix my	סֽוּסָתִי	סֽוּסוֹתַי
2 m.s. " your	סוּסָתְךָ	סֽוּסוֹתֶיךָ
2 f.s. " your	סֽוּסָתֵךְ	סֽוּסוֹתַיִךְ
3 m.s. " his	סֽוּסָתוֹ	סֽוּסוֹתָיו
3 f.s. " her	סֽוּסָתָהּ	סֽוּסוֹתֶיהָ
1 c.p. suffix our	סֽוּסָתֵנוּ	סֽוּסוֹתֵינוּ
2 m.p. " your	סֽוּסַתְכֶם	סוּסֽוֹתֵיכֶם
2 f.p. " your	סֽוּסַתְכֶן	סוּסֽוֹתֵיכֶן
3 m.p. " their	סֽוּסָתָם	סוּסֽוֹתֵיהֶם
3 f.p. " their	סֽוּסָתָן	סוּסֽוֹתֵיהֶן

Note 1: The suffix or its connecting vowel always draws the accent. לְמִינוֹ 1:11 לְמִינֵהוּ 1:12

Note 2: Observe the yôd in all plural nouns before the suffix.

§37. Irregular Nouns with Suffixes

Singular			
Absolute		Construct	With Suffixes
אָב	Father	אֲבִי	אָבִיו or אָבִ֫יהוּ, אָבִ֫יךָ, אָבִי, אָבִ֫יהָ, אֲבִיכֶם
אָח	Brother	אֲחִי	אָחִי, אָחִ֫יךָ, אֲחִיכֶם
אֶחָד	One	אַחַד m. אַחַת f.	
אָחוֹת	Sister	אֲחוֹת	אֲחוֹתִי
אִישׁ	Man	אִישׁ	
אִשָּׁה	Woman	אֵשֶׁת	אִשְׁתִּי, אִשְׁתְּךָ
בַּ֫יִת	House	בֵּית	
בֵּן	Son	בֶּן	בְּנִי, בִּנְךָ
בַּת	Daughter	בַּת	בִּתִּי
יוֹם	Day	יוֹם	
כְּלִי	Vessel		
עִיר	City	עִיר	
פֶּה	Mouth	פִּי	פִּיו or פִּ֫יהוּ, פִּ֫יךָ, פִּי, פִּ֫יהָ, פִּיכֶם
רֹאשׁ	Head	רֹאשׁ	

Plural			
Absolute		Construct	With Suffixes
אָבוֹת	Fathers	אֲבוֹת	
אַחִים	Brothers	אֲחֵי	אֲחֵיכֶם, אַחֶיךָ, אַחַי
אֲחָדִים	Ones		
	Sisters		אַחְוֹתֵיכֶם, אַחְיֹתַי, אַחְיֹתָיו
אֲנָשִׁים	Men	אַנְשֵׁי	
נָשִׁים	Women	נְשֵׁי	נְשֵׁיהֶם, נָשָׁיו
בָּתִּים	Houses	בָּתֵּי	בָּתֵּיהֶם
בָּנִים	Sons	בְּנֵי	בְּנֵיהֶם, בָּנֶיךָ, בָּנַי
בָּנוֹת	Daughters	בְּנוֹת	
יָמִים	Days	יְמֵי	
כֵּלִים	Vessels	כְּלֵי	כְּלֵיהֶם, כֵּלַי
מַיִם	Waters	מֵי	מֵימַי
עָרִים	Cities	עָרֵי	
פִּיּוֹת	Mouths		
רָאשִׁים	Heads	רָאשֵׁי	רָאשֵׁנוּ
שָׁמַיִם	Heavens	שְׁמֵי	

§38. Suffixes Attached to Particles

	מִן from, out	לְ to, for, at	בְּ in, with, by	כְּ like, as
Suffix				
1 c.s.	מִמֶּנִּי	לִי	בִּי	כָּמוֹנִי
2 m.s.	מִמְּךָ	לְךָ	בְּךָ	כָּמוֹךָ
2 f.s.	מִמֵּךְ	לָךְ	בָּךְ	
3 m.s.	מִמֶּנּוּ	לוֹ	בּוֹ	כָּמוֹהוּ
3 f.s.	מִמֶּנָּה	לָהּ	בָּהּ	כָּמוֹהָ
1 c.p.	מִמֶּנּוּ	לָנוּ	בָּנוּ	כָּמוֹנוּ
2 m.p.	מִכֶּם	לָכֶם	בָּכֶם	כָּכֶם
2 f.p.	מִכֶּן	לָכֶן	בָּכֶן	
3 m.p.	מֵהֵמָּה, מֵהֶם	לָהֵמָּה, לָהֶם	בָּהֵמָּה, בָּהֶם, בָּם	כָּהֶם
3 f.p.	מֵהֵנָּה, מֵהֶן	לָהֵנָּה, לָהֶן	בָּהֵנָּה, בָּהֶן	כָּהֵנָּה

Cf. לָהֵן 'therefore'

§39. Pronominal Suffixes Attached to Verbs, Infinitives, and Participles

The suffix as a direct object of the verb may be affixed either directly to the verb or to the accusative particle אֵת. The reflexive noun (myself, himself, etc.) is expressed by the reflexive conjugations Nipʿal and Hitpaʿēl. Puʿal and Hopʿal, since they are passive, do not take a direct object.

1. To the Perfect:

a. In the perfect before suffixes older

אֵת sign of accusative	אֵת with	אֶל to, unto	עַל upon	Suffix
אֹתִי	אִתִּי	אֵלַי	עָלַי	1 c.s.
אֹתְךָ	אִתְּךָ	אֵלֶיךָ	עָלֶיךָ	2 m.s.
אֹתָךְ	אִתָּךְ	אֵלַיִךְ	עָלַיִךְ	2 f.s.
אֹתוֹ	אִתּוֹ	אֵלָיו	עָלָיו	3 m.s.
אֹתָהּ	אִתָּהּ	אֵלֶיהָ	עָלֶיהָ	3 f.s.
אֹתָנוּ	אִתָּנוּ	אֵלֵינוּ	עָלֵינוּ	1 c.p.
אֶתְכֶם	אִתְּכֶם	אֲלֵיכֶם	עֲלֵיכֶם	2 m.p.
אֶתְכֶן	אִתְּכֶן	אֲלֵיכֶן	עֲלֵיכֶן	2 f.p.
אֹתָם	אִתָּם	אֲלֵיהֶם	עֲלֵיהֶם	3 m.p.
אֶתְהֶן	אִתָּן	אֲלֵיהֶן	עֲלֵיהֶן	3 f.p.

verbal afformatives remain:
ת_ for ה ָ 3 f.s.
תִּי for תְּ 2 f.s.
תוּ for תֶּם 2 m.p. (seldom occurs)
To the 3 m.s. is added as a connecting vowel before suffixes an original 'a.' This is pataḥ before נִי, otherwise qāmeṣ. An exception to this rule is ֵךְ, קְטָלֵךְ.

b. The forms which end with a vowel, including those in a. above, take unaccented suffixes. The heavy suffixes כֶם and כֶן are an exception.

Table of suffixes to the

	3 m.s. קָטַל	3 f.s. קָטְלָה	2 m.s. קָטַלְתָּ	2 f.s. קָטַלְתְּ
Suffix				
1 c.s.	קְטָלַנִי	קְטָלַתְנִי	קְטַלְתַּנִי	קְטַלְתִּינִי
2 m.s.	קְטָלְךָ	קְטָלַתְךָ		
2 f.s.	קְטָלֵךְ	קְטָלָתֶךְ		
3 m.s.	קְטָלָהוּ קְטָלוֹ	קְטָלַתְהוּ קְטָלַתּוּ	קְטַלְתָּהוּ קְטַלְתּוֹ	קְטַלְתִּיהוּ
3 f.s.	קְטָלָהּ	קְטָלַתָּה	קְטַלְתָּהּ	קְטַלְתִּיהָ
1 c.p.	קְטָלָנוּ	קְטָלַתְנוּ	קְטַלְתָּנוּ	קְטַלְתִּינוּ
2 m.p.				
3 m.p.	קְטָלָם	קְטָלָתַם	קְטַלְתָּם	קְטַלְתִּים
3 f.p.	קְטָלָן	קְטָלָתַן		

Note 1: 3 m.s. suffix הוּ with connecting qāmeṣ forms ָהוּ which may contract to ḥōlem (וֹ).

Note 2: 3 m.s. suffix הוּ with connecting ḥîreq yô<u>d</u> forms *ִיהוּ which regularly contracts to ִיו.

Note 3: 3 m.s. suffix הוּ joined to 3 f.s. afformative ת_ forms ַתְהוּ_ which may contract to ַתּוּ_.

Note 4: 3 f.s. suffix הָ with connecting qāmeṣ forms *ָהָ which regularly becomes ָהּ.

Note 5: 3 f.s. suffix הָ joined to 3 f.s. afformative ת_ forms *ַתְהָ_ which becomes ַתָּה_.

Note 6: 2 f.s. suffix ךְ joined to the 3 f.s. af-

<u>perfect of the strong verb</u>

1 c.s. קְטַלְתִּי	3 c.p. קְטָלוּ	2 m.p. קְטַלְתֶּם	1 c.p. קְטַלְנוּ	Suffix
	קְטָלוּנִי	קְטַלְתּוּנִי		1 c.s.
קְטַלְתִּיךָ	קְטָלוּךָ		קְטַלְנוּךָ	2 m.s.
קְטַלְתִּיךְ	קְטָלוּךְ		קְטַלְנוּךְ	2 f.s.
קְטַלְתִּיו קְטַלְתִּיהוּ	קְטָלוּהוּ	קְטַלְתּוּהוּ	קְטַלְנוּהוּ	3 m.s.
קְטַלְתִּיהָ	קְטָלוּהָ		קְטַלְנוּהָ	3 f.s.
	קְטָלוּנוּ	קְטַלְתּוּנוּ		1 c.p.
קְטַלְתִּיכֶם			קְטַלְנוּכֶם	2 m.p.
קְטַלְתִּים	קְטָלוּם	קְטַלְתּוּם	קְטַלְנוּם	3 m.p.
קְטַלְתִּין	קְטָלוּן			3 f.p.

formative ת_ forms *תְךְ_ which becomes תֶךָ.

Note 7: 3 m. and f. p. suffixes ם and ן joined to the 3 f.s. afformative form תָם and תָן. Observe the assimilated ה in the forms mentioned in notes 3 and 5: תּוּ, תָּה.

2. To the Imperfect:

a. Imperfect forms having an afformative take unaccented suffixes.

b. Imperfect forms having no afformative take an accented ṣērē as the connecting vowel. The exceptions are ךָ, ךְ, כֶם, כֶן.

<u>Table of suffixes to the</u>

	3 m.s. יִקְטֹל	3 f.s. תִּקְטֹל	2 m.s. תִּקְטֹל	2 f.s. תִּקְטְלִי	1 c.s. אֶקְטֹל
Suffix					
1 c.s.	יִקְטְלֵנִי				
2 m.s.	יִקְטָלְךָ				
2 f.s.	יִקְטְלֵךְ				
3 m.s.	יִקְטְלֵהוּ				
3 f.s.	יִקְטְלֶהָ יִקְטְלָהּ				
1 c.p.	יִקְטְלֵנוּ				
2 m.p.	יִקְטָלְכֶם				
3 m.p.	יִקְטְלֵם				

The vocalization of the 3 f.s., 2 m.s., 2 f.s., 1 c.s., and 1 c.p. is the same as the 3 m.s.; that of the 2 m.p. and 2 f.p. the same as 3 f.p.

Note 1: The ḥōlem of the imperfect Qal becomes qāmeṣ ḥāṭûp̱ before the 2 m.s. and p. suffix; otherwise it reduces to shewa (the imperfect does not occur with the suffix כֶן).

Note 2: Imperfects with pataḥ instead of ḥōlem retain the "a" type vowel before suffixes rather than reducing to shewa. The ḥîreq yôḏ of Hip̱ʿîl is also retained.

Note 3: The feminine plural ending נָה before suffixes is replaced by the masculine plural end-

<u>imperfect of the strong verb</u>

3 m.p. יִקְטְלוּ	3 f.p. תִּקְטֹלְנָה	2 m.p. תִּקְטְלוּ	2 f.p. תִּקְטֹלְנָה	1 c.p. נִקְטֹל	
					Suffix
יִקְטְלוּנִי	תִּקְטְלוּנִי				1 c.s.
יִקְטְלוּךָ					2 m.s.
יִקְטְלוּךְ					2 f.s.
יִקְטְלוּהוּ	תִּקְטְלוּהוּ				3 m.s.
יִקְטְלוּהָ	תִּקְטְלוּהָ				3 f.s.
יִקְטְלוּנוּ	תִּקְטְלוּנוּ				1 c.p.
יִקְטָלוּכֶם					2 m.p.
יִקְטְלוּם	תִּקְטְלוּם				3 m.p.

ing וּ (usually אֵת plus the pronominal suffix is used instead of these forms).

3. To the Imperative:
   a. The 2 m.s. imperative Qal before suffixes is *קָטְל (qoṭl).
   b. The suffixes occur with the same connecting vowel as in the imperfect.
   c. Imperatives with pataḥ as the thematic vowel retain the "a" type vowel before suffixes.

<u>Table of suffixes to the imperative of the strong verb</u>

	2 m.s. קְטֹל	2 f.s. קִטְלִי	2 m.p. קִטְלוּ	2 f.p. קְטֹלְנָה
Suffix				
1 c.s.	קָטְלֵנִי		קִטְלוּנִי	
2 m.s.				
2 f.s.				
3 m.s.	קָטְלֵהוּ		קִטְלוּהוּ	
3 f.s.	קָטְלָהּ		קִטְלוּהָ	
1 c.p.	קָטְלֵנוּ		קִטְלוּנוּ	
2 m.p.			etc.	
2 f.p.				
3 m.p.	קָטְלֵם			
3 f.p.				
	From an imperfect with paṯaḥ			
1 c.s.	שְׁלַחֵנִי		שִׁלְחוּנִי	

4. To the Infinitive Construct:
   a. Since the infinitive construct is a noun, it takes the pronominal suffixes in the same manner as the noun.
   b. The Qal infinitive construct before pronominal suffixes is normally *קָטְל (qoṭl). Before the suffixes ךָ, כֶם, כֶן, the Qal infinitive construct may appear either as *קָטְל (qoṭl) or *קְטָל (q^{e}ṭol).
   c. The first syllable before vocalic suffixes is almost always loosely closed (i.e., a following begaḏkep̱aṯ consonant does not bear a dāḡēš lēnē), e.g., עָמְדָה; before consonantal suffixes, however, it is firmly closed, e.g., שָׁפְכְּךָ.
   d. The infinitive construct with its suffix is a construct relation and may be either

subjective (קָטְלְךָ 'your killing') or objective (קָטְלְךָ 'killing you'). A difference in form occurs only in the 1 c.s. suffix, e.g., subjective קָטְלִי, objective קָטְלֵנִי.

Note: The infinitive absolute never takes a suffix.

Table of suffixes to the infinitive construct

קְטֹל		קְטֹל	
Suffix		Suffix	
1 c.s.	קָטְלִי, קָטְלֵנִי	1 c.p.	קָטְלֵנוּ
2 m.s.	קָטְלְךָ, קְטָלְךָ	2 m.p.	קָטְלְכֶם
2 f.s.	קָטְלֵךְ	2 f.p.	קָטְלְכֶן
3 m.s.	קָטְלוֹ	3 m.p.	קָטְלָם
3 f.s.	קָטְלָהּ	3 f.p.	קָטְלָן

5. Table of Qal participles, s. and p., with suffixes

	m.s.	f.s. part.	m.p.	f.p. part.
Abs.	קֹטֵל	קֹטְלָה or קֹטֶלֶת	קֹטְלִים	קֹטְלוֹת
Const.	קֹטֵל	קֹטְלַת or קֹטֶלֶת	קֹטְלֵי	קֹטְלוֹת
1 c.s.	קֹטְלִי	קֹטְלָתִי	קֹטְלַי	קֹטְלוֹתַי
2 m.s.	קֹטֶלְךָ	קֹטְלָתְךָ	קֹטְלֶיךָ	קֹטְלוֹתֶיךָ
2 f.s.	קֹטְלֵךְ	קֹטְלָתֵךְ	קֹטְלַיִךְ	קֹטְלוֹתַיִךְ
3 m.s.	קֹטְלוֹ	קֹטְלָתוֹ	קֹטְלָיו	קֹטְלוֹתָיו
3 f.s.	קֹטְלָהּ	קֹטְלָתָהּ	קֹטְלֶיהָ	קֹטְלוֹתֶיהָ
1 c.p.	קֹטְלֵנוּ	קֹטְלָתֵנוּ	קֹטְלֵינוּ	קֹטְלוֹתֵינוּ
2 m.p.	קֹטֶלְכֶם	קֹטְלַתְכֶם	קֹטְלֵיכֶם	קֹטְלוֹתֵיכֶם
2 f.p.	קֹטֶלְכֶן	קֹטְלַתְכֶן	קֹטְלֵיכֶן	קֹטְלוֹתֵיכֶן
3 m.p.	קֹטְלָם	קֹטְלָתָם	קֹטְלֵיהֶם	קֹטְלוֹתֵיהֶם
3 f.p.	קֹטְלָן	קֹטְלָתָן	קֹטְלֵיהֶן	קֹטְלוֹתֵיהֶן

Note: The participle may also be united to suffixes with the same connecting vowel as in the imperfect verb.

§40. The Nûn Energicum (Energetic Nûn)

The imperfect is sometimes strengthened before the suffixes נִי, ךָ, הוּ, and הָ by the addition of an accented ֶן (original ַן).

יִקְטְלַנִּי or יִקְטְלֶנִּי (ַנְנִי- > ַנִּי-; ֶנְנִי > ֶנִּי)

יִקְטְלֶךָּ (ֶנְךָ > ֶךָּ, sometimes written ֶכָּה)

יִקְטְלֶנּוּ (ֶנְהוּ > ֶנּוּ)

יִקְטְלֶנָּה (ֶנְהָ > ֶנָּה)

יִקְטְלֶנּוּ (ֶנְנוּ > ֶנּוּ)

Note 1: Nûn energicum does not occur with other suffixes.

Note 2: Before the suffixes נִי, ךָ, and נוּ, the nûn is assimilated to the following consonant.

Note 3: The ה of the 3rd sing. suffixes is assimilated back into the nûn.

Note 4: The 3 m.s. and 1 c.p. suffixes with nûn energicum are not distinguishable except by context. The 1 c.p. almost never occurs. תְּשׁוּפֶנּוּ 3:15

§41. The Adjective

The adjective may be either attributive or predicative.

1. The attributive adjective:
   a. The attributive adjective directly qualifies its noun as a modifier, e.g., 'the good man.'
   b. The attributive adjective agrees with its noun in number, gender, and definiteness.
      אִישׁ טוֹב 'a good man'
      הָאִישׁ הַטּוֹב 'the good man'
      אִשָּׁה טוֹבָה 'a good woman'
      הָאִשָּׁה הַטּוֹבָה 'the good woman'
   c. The attributive adjective usually follows its noun.

d. When an attributive adjective qualifies a noun in the construct state:

1) It necessarily follows the absolute since no word may come between a construct and its absolute.

2) It agrees with the definiteness of the construct.

3) When the absolute and construct are of the same number and gender, the attributive adjective may qualify either; context is the determining factor.

אֵ֫שֶׁת הָאִישׁ הַטּוֹבָה 'the good wife of the man'

סוּס הָאִישׁ הַטּוֹב 'the good horse of the man'
'the horse of the good man'

2. The predicate adjective:

a. The predicate adjective qualifies its noun after a copula, e.g., 'the man is good.'

Note: The verb 'to be' as a copula does not exist in Hebrew. The personal pronoun may often serve as a copula, e.g., 2:19, 14:8, 23:19

b. The predicate adjective agrees with its noun in number and gender, but is never definite.

טוֹב הָאִישׁ 'The man (is) good'

טוֹבָה הָאִשָּׁה 'The woman (is) good'

c. The predicate adjective usually precedes its noun. Observe that only the context will determine whether טוֹב אִישׁ means 'a good man' or 'a man is good.'

Note: The singular adjective forms its plural with the regular plural endings. Adjectives never take the dual ending.

m.s. טוֹב	f.s. טוֹבָה
m.p. טוֹבִים	f.p. טוֹבוֹת

3. Degrees of comparison:
   a. The comparative degree is either expressed by מִן (cf. §70.4.b) or is implied from the context.
   b. The superlative degree is expressed:
      1) By the attributive adjective after a definite noun, e.g., בְּנוֹ הַגָּדוֹל 'his oldest son,' i.e., 'his son, the oldest one.'
      2) By placing the adjective in the construct state before a definite noun, e.g., קְטוֹן בָּנָיו 'his youngest son,' i.e., 'the young one of his sons.'

§42. The Demonstrative Pronoun

	Singular		Plural	
m.	זֶה	this	אֵלֶּה (אֵל)	these
f.	זֹאת			
	(זֹה, זוֹ	rare forms)		
m.	הוּא	that	הֵמָּה, הֵם	those
f.	הִיא		הֵנָּה, הֵן	

1. The demonstrative may be either attributive or predicative.
2. The attributive demonstrative is always definite and follows its noun.
3. The predicative demonstrative never takes the article.
   הָאִישׁ הַטּוֹב הַזֶּה 'this good man'
   זֶה הָאִישׁ הַטּוֹב 'this (is) the good man'

Note 1: The article retains its original demonstrative force with some words of time as: הַיּוֹם 'today,' הַלַּיְלָה 'tonight,' and with other words relating to time.

Note 2: כֹּל when followed by a definite noun is translated "all"; when followed by an indefinite noun, it is translated "every."

§43. The Interrogative Pronoun

מִי 'who?' מָה, מַה, מֶה 'what?' ('how?' 'why?')

מִי normally stands independently; מָה is usually joined to the following word by maqqēp̱ or a conjunctive accent.

1. Before strong letters (not laryngeals) it is written מַה plus following dāg̱ēš forte, e.g., מַה־יִּקְרָא 2:19 מַה־זֹּאת 3:13
2. Before א, ע, ר, and in pause, it is written מָה־, e.g., מָה־אֵלֶּה.
3. Before ה, ח, ע, when they bear a qāmeṣ, it is written מֶה־, e.g., מֶה עָשִׂיתָ 4:10
4. Before ה, ח, ע, when bearing a vowel other than qāmeṣ, it may be written מַה־, מֶה־, מָה־, e.g., מַה־הִיא, מָה־הַמָּה.

Note: Observe the following frequently used interrogatives:

לָמָּה 'why?'	מָתַי 'when?'
אַיֵּה 'where?'	אֵי־זֶה 'which?'
מֵאַיִן or אֵי מִזֶּה 'whence?'	אָנָה 'whither?'

§44. Hê Interrogative

The simple question is normally introduced by the particle הֲ, prefixed to the first word in the sentence, which may be a noun, verb, or particle.

It is pointed:

1. Before strong letters (not laryngeals) which bear a full vowel (i.e., not vocal shewa), הֲ.
   הֲמִן 3:11
2. Before consonants which bear shewa, הַ.
   הַמְכַסֶּה 18:17
   Occasionally dāg̱ēš forte will follow הַ.
   הַלְּבֶן 17:17
3. Before laryngeals which bear qames, הֶ.
   הֶהָשֵׁב 24:5

4. Before laryngeals which bear vowels other than qāmeṣ, הַ. הַאֲלֵךְ.

Note: The interrogative sentence, however, may occur without an interrogative particle. The context must determine the interrogative character of the statement.

§45. The Relative Pronoun

The relative pronoun is the indeclinable אֲשֶׁר. Occasionally the relative is שֶׁ or שַׁ with following dāg̱ēš forte, especially in late Hebrew.

§46. Hê Terminative

"Direction toward" or "motion toward" may be expressed in Hebrew by appending an unaccented הָ to the singular noun. Some grammarians consider this הָ to be an old accusative ending. הַנֶּגְבָּה 12:9

§47. The Irregular Verbs

Irregular verbs are those:

- which have in their root one or more of the following consonants: the laryngeals, yôḏ, or wāw.
- which have nûn as their first consonant.
- whose second and third consonants are identical.

In Hebrew grammar the conjugations are named on the basis of the root פעל; accordingly, the consonants פ, ע, and ל are used to indicate the first, second, and third positions of radicals in the root. Thus the first radical of any root is called the "פ" radical, the second the "ע" radical, and the third the "ל" radical.

The irregular verbs are listed as follows:

1. Laryngeal verbs:
   a. פ laryngeal: verbs beginning with a laryngeal, e.g., חבש, עבד
   b. ע laryngeal: verbs whose second radical is a laryngeal, e.g., צעק, שאל
   c. ל laryngeal: verbs whose final radical is a laryngeal, e.g., שמע, שלח
2. Weak verbs:
   a. Pê ʾĀlep (פ"א). Five verbs, אבד, אבה, אכל, אמר, אפה, belong to this class. All other verbs beginning with א belong to the פ laryngeal class.
   b. Lāmed Hê (ל"ה), e.g., בנה, גלה
   c. Lāmed ʾĀlep (ל"א), e.g., קרא, מצא
   d. Pê Yôd (פ"י), e.g., יצא, ילד, ישב
   e. Pê Nûn (פ"ן), e.g., נפל, נתן
   f. ʿAyin Wāw, ʿAyin Yôd (ע"ו, ע"י) (hollow verbs), e.g., אור, מות
   g. ʿAyin ʿAyin (ע"ע) (double Ayin), e.g., סבב, רעע
   h. Doubly weak, i.e., more than one weak radical in the root, e.g., נטה, עשה, ידה, נשא

The vocalization of the strong verb is basic to the Hebrew verbal system. Any vowel deviation in an irregular verb from the vocalization of the strong verb may be explained as resulting from the peculiarities inherent in the weak radicals. Thus a mastery of the strong verb together with a knowledge of the peculiarities of weak radicals will enable the student to master the irregular verb.

Laryngeal verbs: The vocalization of the laryngeal verbs differs from that of the strong verb because of the peculiarity of the laryngeal. Cf. §13.

§48. <u>The פ Laryngeal Verb</u>

1. Since the laryngeal prefers a compound shewa, the following changes from the strong verb occur:

   a. Simple vocal shewa becomes compound shewa, usually ḥāṭēp̱ paṯaḥ. Cf. קְטַלְתֶּם with עֲמַדְתֶּם.

   b. Silent shewa which closed the syllable in the strong verb becomes compound shewa, thus opening the syllable. The vowel of this syllable then becomes a short vowel corresponding to the vowel of the compound shewa and normally receives a meteg. Cf. יִקְטֹל with יַעֲמֹד.

   c. Before vocalic afformatives or pronominal suffixes, the second radical of the root bears vocal shewa, e.g., יִקְטְלוּ. Correspondingly, the root עמד would appear *יַעֲמְדוּ. Since, however, two vocal shewas cannot stand together, the consonant with compound shewa takes the short vowel corresponding to the vowel of the compound shewa, e.g., יַעַמְדוּ; וַיַּהַרְגֵהוּ 4:8.

   Observe the shewa <u>medium</u> in these forms. Cf. §8.note 5.

Note 1: In the Qal imperfect when the thematic vowel is ḥōlem, the preformative vowel is usually paṯaḥ, e.g., יַעֲמֹד; when the thematic vowel is paṯaḥ, the preformative vowel is usually sᵉg̱ôl, e.g., יֶאֱזַב.

Note 2: The preformative א of the Qal imperfect always has sᵉg̱ôl, e.g., אֶעֱמֹד.

Note 3: The laryngeal sometimes appears with simple vocal shewa, e.g., יֶהְיֶה 1:29.

Note 4: The preformative vowel of Nip̱ʽal perfect and participle and Hip̱ʽîl perfect is segôl, e.g., נֶעֱמַד, הֶעֱמִיד.

Note 5: Observe that in the Hop'al the regular preformative vowel (qāmeṣ ḥāṭûp) causes the laryngeal to bear ḥāṭēp qāmeṣ, e.g., יָעֳמַד.

2. Since the laryngeals refuse to be doubled, the previous vowel must be lengthened in compensation. This occurs in the פ laryngeal verbs only in the Nip'al imperfect, imperative, and infinitives, e.g., יֵעָמֵד.
Cf. יִקָּטֵל with יֵעָמֵד. וַתֵּרָאֶה 1:9

§49. The ע Laryngeal Verb

1. Since the laryngeal prefers compound shewa, wherever the radical of the strong verb has vocal shewa, the laryngeals (א, ה, ח, ע) take compound shewa (ֲ). Cf. קָטְלָה with בָּחֲרָה.

Note: The Qal imperfect and imperative take paṯaḥ as the thematic vowel, e.g., יִבְחַר, בְּחַר. The infinitive, however, retains ḥōlem, e.g., בְּחֹר, בָּחוֹר.

2. Since the laryngeal rejects dāgēš forte, the doubling of the middle radical of the intensives (Pi'ēl, Pu'al, Hiṯpa'ēl) cannot take place. Thus:

a. Always before ר, frequently before א and ע, the vowel is lengthened (ḥîreq to ṣērē, paṯaḥ to qāmeṣ, qibbûṣ to ḥōlem).

b. Since ה and ח are doubled by implication (cf. §13.1.b), the previous vowel does not change.

Note: The thematic vowel of the Pi'ēl perfect 3 m.s. is usually ṣērē; with א and ע it is always ṣērē; with ה, ח, and ר it is more frequently paṯaḥ.

§50. The ל Laryngeal Verb

To this class belong only those verbs ending in ה, ח, and ע.

1. Pataḥ furtive appears after originally long 'i' or 'u' class vowels. Cf. קָטוּל with שָׁלוּחַ.
2. Since the laryngeal prefers the 'a' class vowel, the thematic vowel of the Qal imperfect is always pataḥ, e.g., יִשְׁלַח. The thematic vowel of other conjugations in the imperfect (except Hip̄ʿîl) is usually pataḥ.

   Note 1: The ṣērē of the Qal active participle becomes pataḥ in construct:

   abs. זֹבֵחַ const. זֹבַח

   Note 2: The ṣērē of the Hip̄ʿîl jussive or Hip̄ʿîl with wāw consecutive, or of the Hip̄ʿîl imperative, becomes pataḥ, e.g., וַיַּשְׁלַח.
3. The laryngeal bears silent shewa before consonantal afformatives.

   Note: 2 f.s. perfect takes a helping pataḥ instead of shewa, e.g., שָׁלַחַתְּ. The afformative תְּ retains its dāḡēš lēnē and silent shewa.

Weak verbs: The laryngeal verbs differ from the strong verb only in vocalization. They are, therefore, only a variety of the strong verb; the consonants of the weak verb, on the other hand, may quiesce (lose their consonantal value), contract, elide, or be assimilated.

§51. The פ"א Verb

The פ"א verb shares all the peculiarities of the פ laryngeal verb except in the Qal imperfect of the five verbs: אבד 'to perish,' אבה 'to be willing,' אכל 'to eat,' אמר 'to say,' אפה 'to bake.'

1. In the Qal imperfect of these five verbs the א quiesces and coalesces with the vowel of the preformative to form an open syllable.

   The ḥîreq of the preformative in יִקְטֹל was originally a paṯaḥ. Cf. §23.1.a.note. Thus the presumed original form of the 3 m.s. of אמר was *יַאְמַר. Since, however, the א does not close a syllable, it thereby causes the original paṯaḥ to become qāmeṣ. Cf. §13.note. *יַאְמַר > *יָאמַר. In an early period this qāmeṣ became ḥōlem, e.g., *יָאמַר > יֹאמַר. וַיֹּאמֶר 1:3

2. The א of the 1 c.s. imperfect coalesces with the א of the root, e.g., *אאכַל > אֹכַל. וָאֹכֵל 3:12

   Note 1: The infinitive construct of אמר regularly appears with the preposition לְ, thus: לֵאמֹר. This word normally introduces direct discourse.

   לְ+אֱמֹר > *לֶאֱמֹר > *לְאמֹר > לֵאמֹר

   Note 2: The verbs אהב 'to love' and אחז 'to seize' are occasionally conjugated in the same manner as the five verbs mentioned above.

§52. The ל"ה Verb

The so-called ל"ה verbs are in reality either ל"ו or ל"י, of which ל"ו has virtually disappeared from Hebrew. The yôḏ of the ל"י verb disappears in all forms without afformatives and is replaced by ה, hence the designation 'ל"ה' verb.

The verb is inflected as follows:

1. Without afformatives:
   a. All perfects end in ָה.
   b. All imperfects end in ֶה.
   c. All imperatives end in ֵה.
   d. All participles end in ֶה (except Qal passive גָּלוּי). In construct they become ֵה.

e. All infinitives construct end in וֹת.

f. All infinitives absolute end in ֹה except Hip̱ʻîl, Hop̱ʻal, and generally Piʻēl, which end in ֵה.

2. With vocalic afformatives:

a. The yôḏ with its preceding vowel or shewa disappears before vocalic afformatives or suffixes.

Cf. קָטְלוּ with גָּלוּ (original *גָּלְיוּ)

Cf. תִּקְטְלִי with תִּגְלִי (original *תִּגְלְיִי)

Cf. יִקְטְלֵנִי with יִגְלֵנִי (original *יִגְלְיֵנִי)

b. The 3 f.s. perfect is formed by adding the old feminine afformative ת to the stem, to which is added redundantly ָה.

(*גָּלְיַת < *גָּלָת < גָּלְתָה) הָיְתָה 1:2

3. With consonantal afformatives:

Before consonantal afformatives the original yôḏ is retained as the third radical. This yôḏ with its preceding vowel (thus an original diphthong, cf. *גָּלַיְתָּ) appears:

a. In the perfect Qal as ḥîreq yôḏ, e.g., גָּלִיתָ.

b. In the perfect Puʻal and Hop̱ʻal as ṣērē yôḏ, e.g., גֻּלֵּיתָ, הָגְלֵיתָ.

c. In the perfects of other conjugations either as ḥîreq yôḏ or ṣērē yôḏ.

d. In all imperatives and imperfects as s^e^g̱ôl yôḏ, e.g., תִּגְלֶינָה.

4. In the jussive or imperfect with waw consecutive, in forms without suffixes or afformatives, the ה is apocopated (lit., cut away').

a. Puʻal and Hop̱ʻal apocopated forms do not occur.

b. Nip̱ʻal, Piʻēl, and Hiṯpaʻēl are apocopated without further change, except the dropping of dāg̱ēš forte from Piʻēl and

Hitpa'ēl.
תִּגָּלֶה<תִּגָּל , or with waw consecutive וַתִּגָּל
יְכַלֶּה<יְכַל , or with waw consecutive וַיְכַל
יִתְגַּלֶּה<יִתְגַּל , or with wāw consecutive וַיִּתְגַּל. וַיְצַו 2:16

Note: Observe that a final consonant does not bear dāgēš forte (except the personal pronoun אַתְּ).

c. When Qal is apocopated there remains a doubly closed syllable, e.g., יִגְלֶה<*יִגְלְ. This apocopated form appears:

1) sometimes unchanged, e.g., וַיַּרְא 1:4; וַיִּשְׁבְּ.
2) sometimes with a lengthened vowel, e.g., וָאֵשְׁתְּ 24:46 וַיֵּבְךְּ 27:38 וַיֵּשְׁתְּ 9:21.
3) with a helping vowel, e.g., וַיִּבֶן 2:22 יִרֶב 1:22.
   a פ laryngeal with a helping vowel, e.g., וַיַּעַשׂ 1:7 וַתַּהַר 4:1 וַיִּחַר 4:5 תַּעַשׂ 22:12
4) with a lengthening and a helping vowel, e.g., וַתֵּרֶא 3:6.

d. When Hip'îl is apocopated there remains a doubly closed syllable, e.g., יַרְאֶה appears with wāw consecutive as וַיַּרְא. This apocopated form appears sometimes:

1) unchanged, e.g., יַפְתְּ 9:27 וַיַּשְׁקְ 29:10
2) with a helping vowel, e.g., וַיֶּפֶן, וַיֶּגֶל.
   פ laryngeal with a helping vowel, e.g., וַיַּעַל, וַיַּעַן, וַיַּעַשׂ (these forms are exactly like Qal).

Note: The jussive and wāw consecutive forms of היה and חיה are inflected irregularly. The 3 m.s. imperfect Qal is יִהְיֶה and יִחְיֶה. The jussive of these forms would be the unpronounceable *יִהְיְ and *יִחְיְ,

which become יְהִי and יְחִי. The imperfect with wāw consecutive appears וַיְהִי and וַיְחִי. Note Genesis 1:3.

5. In the imperative:

Piʻēl, Hitpaʻēl, and Hipʻîl imperatives are rarely apocopated: צַו for צַוֵּה, גַּל for גַּלֵּה, הִתְחַל for הִתְחַלֵּה. The apocopated Hipʻîl imperative always has a helping vowel, e.g., הַרְבֵּה < הַרְבְּ* < הֶרֶב ; הַעֲלֵה < הַעַל.

Note: The infinitive absolute Hipʻîl of רבה is either הַרְבָּה or הַרְבֵּה. הַרְבֵּה is generally used adverbially.

6. With the cohortative:

The regular form of the imperfect ending in הֶ serves also in the first person to express the cohortative, e.g., נַעֲשֶׂה 1:26.

§53. <u>The ל"א Verb</u>

The ל"א verb exhibits the following peculiarities:

1. Final א always quiesces. This quiescent א causes a preceding pataḥ to be lengthened to qāmeṣ. This occurs only in Qal perfect, imperfect, imperative; Nipʻal perfect; and the entire Puʻal and Hopʻal.

   בָּרָא 1:1   וַיִּקְרָא   קָרָא 1:5

2. Before vocalic afformatives א maintains its consonantal value since every syllable must begin with a consonant. Cf. §7.1.

3. Before consonantal afformatives א quiesces.

   a. In the perfect, the previous vowel is lengthened.

   b. In the imperfect and imperative, the previous vowel is s^{e}gôl.

Note: The infinitive construct occasionally takes the ending ת on the analogy of the ל"ה verb, e.g., לִקְרָאת 15:10.

§54. The פ"י Verb

There are two classes of פ"י verbs, those with
original yôḏ and those with original wāw. Without
preformatives all these verbs appear with the yôḏ.
1. Verbs with original wāw: this wāw after pre-
    formatives is either rejected, or retained as
    yôḏ or wāw.
    a. The wāw is rejected in the Qal imperfect,
        imperative, and infinitive construct in
        the following eight words: ילד 'to bring
        forth,' יצא 'to go forth,' ישב 'to sit'
        or 'to dwell,' ירד 'to descend,' הלך 'to
        go' (see note), ידע 'to know,' יחד 'to be
        united,' יקע 'to be dislocated.'
        1) The thematic vowel of the imperfect is
            ṣērē; before laryngeals the vowel is
            paṯaḥ.
        2) The preformative vowel is unchangeable
            ṣērē.
        3) When the preformative is dropped, as
            in the imperative, only two radicals
            of the root remain.
        4) To the infinitive construct is added a
            ת, thus forming a segolate (cf. §60).

Perfect	יָלַד	יָצָא	יָדַע	הָלַךְ
Imperfect	יֵלֵד	יֵצֵא	יֵדַע	יֵלֵךְ
Imperative	לֵד	צֵא	דַּע	לֵךְ
Inf. Const.	לֶדֶת	צֵאת	דַּעַת	לֶכֶת

    Note: The verb הלך is inflected in the
           Qal imperfect, imperative, infini-
           tive construct, and Hipˁîl perfect
           and imperfect as though it were יָלַךְ.
    b. The wāw is retained as yôḏ in the Qal im-
        perfect, imperative, and infinitive con-
        struct of some verbs (usually intransi-
        tive), e.g., יבש 'to be dry,' ירא 'to be

afraid,' ירשׁ 'to possess,' ישׁן 'to sleep.'

Perfect	יָבֵשׁ	יָרֵא	יָרַשׁ
Imperfect	יִיבַשׁ	יִירָא	יִירַשׁ
Imperative	יְבַשׁ	יְרָא	רֵשׁ, יְרַשׁ
Inf. Const.	יְבֹשׁ, יְבֹשֶׁת	יְרֹא	רֶשֶׁת

(The wāw may be retained as yôd in the imperfect and participles of the intensives.)

c. The wāw appears:

1) As a consonant in the Nip̱ʻal imperfect, imperative, and infinitives and sometimes in the imperfect, infinitives, and participles of the intensives.

2) As ḥōlem (וֹ) in Nip̱ʻal perfect and participle and throughout Hip̱ʻîl, e.g., וַתּוֹצֵא 1:12.

3) As šûreq throughout Hop̱ʻal.

2. Verbs with original yôd are the following: יטב 'to be good,' ילל (only Hip̱ʻîl) 'to howl,' ימן (only Hip̱ʻîl) 'to go right,' ינק 'to suck,' יקץ 'to awaken,' ישׁר 'to be straight.'

a. These verbs are distinguishable from the verbs with original waw only in Hip̱ʻîl, where the yôd remains after the preformative, e.g., תֵּיטִיב 4:6.

b. The yôd is always present in the Qal imperfect where it coalesces with the ḥîreq of the preformative.

Note 1: Observe the defective writing of ḥîreq yôd in 2:19, וַיִּצֶר for וַיִּיצֶר.

Note 2: In a few פ"ו verbs the wāw is assimilated to the second radical (usually צ) of the root as the ן of פ"ן verbs. Cf. §55. *יִוְצֹק > יִצֹּק 28:13. Other verbs with this peculiarity are יצג, יצע, יצת. Cf. Gesenius-Kautzsch, §71.

Note 3: Observe the following:

a. The imperfect of יכל, 'to be able,' is יוּכַל. This imperfect form is considered by some grammarians to be a Hop̱ʻal, by others a passive of Qal.

b. יהב, 'to give,' occurs (only in the imperative Qal) as an expletive, with the usual meaning 'Come.' הַב, הָבָה, הָבִי, הָבוּ. Observe the occurrence of these words in Gen. 11:3,4,7; 29:21; 30:1; 38:16; 47:16.

§55. <u>The פ"ן Verb</u>

The weakness of the פ"ן is the tendency of the ן to be assimilated to the following consonant whenever possible.

1. The ן is assimilated to the second radical whenever the ן with the preformative forms a closed syllable. Thus:
   a. Qal imperfect
      יִפֹּל < *יִנְפֹּל
   b. Nip̱ʻal perfect and participle
      נִפָּל < *נִנְפָּל , נִפַּל < *נִנְפַּל
   c. Entire Hip̱ʻîl and Hop̱ʻal
      הִפִּיל < *הִנְפִּיל etc.
      הֻפַּל < *הָנְפַּל Observe qibbûṣ. Cf. §21.1.a. note.

2. The ן is dropped ('aphaeresis'):
   a. In all Qal imperatives whose imperfect thematic vowel is paṯaḥ, e.g., גַּשׁ < *נְגַשׁ.
   b. Usually in the Qal infinitive construct of those verbs whose imperfect thematic vowel is paṯaḥ. The resulting form is lengthened by the addition of a ת to form a segolate. Cf. §60.

   Note: Observe the similarity of these forms to those mentioned in §54.1.a.4.

3. The נ is retained:
   a. In verbs which are both פ"ן and ע laryngeal, e.g., נחם, נחל.
   b. In Qal imperative and infinitive construct of verbs whose thematic vowel is ḥōlem.
   c. In all forms where נ bears a vowel or vocal shewa.

Note 1: The verb לקח, 'to take,' is treated in the Qal as though it were פ"ן. In the Qal imperative and infinitive construct the ל is dropped.
לָקַח 2:22 יִקַּח 2:15 קַח 6:21 קַחַת 4:11
(לָקַחַת < לְ+קַחַת)
The form יֻקַּח 18:4, 12:15 is explained as either Hopʻal imperfect or Qal passive imperfect.

Note 2: The verb נתן:
   a. Takes as its Qal imperfect thematic vowel a ṣērē.
   b. Loses its final nûn by assimilation before consonantal afformatives (refer to paradigm).
   c. Drops initial nûn in Qal imperative and infinitive construct (refer to paradigm). For the addition of suffixes to the Qal infinitive construct see the section on the segolate noun, §60.

§56. The ע"י and ע"ו Verbs (Hollow Verbs)

The peculiarity of the hollow verb is that its middle radical (י or ו) never (except in rare forms of Piʻēl) has consonantal force and often disappears. The few verbs whose second radical is consonantal yôḏ or wāw are not hollow verbs, e.g., צוה, היה, חיה, קוה, גוע. The dictionary form of the hollow verb is always the Qal infinitive construct since the middle radical disappears in Qal perfect.

The verb is inflected as follows:

1. The yôḏ or wāw never appears in the Qal perfect or Qal active participle (except in some stative verbs). The 3 m.s. perfect is קָם, perhaps from an original *קָוַם. The active participle is also קָם. Before consonantal afformatives in the Qal perfect the vowel is paṯaḥ.

   Note: The Qal perfect of the ע"י is vocalized the same as ע"ו, e.g., בָּן, בָּנָה, etc., from the verb בִּין.

2. The original short vowel of the preformatives in Qal imperfect, Nip̱ʻal perfect and participle, and the entire Hip̱ʻîl and Hop̱ʻal must be lengthened when it stands in an open unaccented syllable. The thematic vowel is irregular. Cf. paradigm.

3. The vocalic afformatives do <u>not</u> draw the accent, except in the Hop̱ʻal. Cf. קָטְלָה with קָמָה; קָטְלוּ with קָמוּ.

4. Before consonantal afformatives except in the Qal perfect a helping vowel is often inserted to preserve the ִי or ו of the stem. Cf. §30.1.note 2.

   a. In the Nip̱ʻal and Hip̱ʻîl perfect the helping vowel is ḥōlem. This ḥōlem is accented before light consonantal afformatives (i.e., not before תֶּם and תֶּן).

      Note: The accented helping ḥōlem of Nip̱ʻal perfect causes the previous ḥōlem to become šûreq in forms which have a light consonantal afformative.

   b. In the imperfect Qal and sometimes Hip̱ʻîl the helping vowel is accented ֶי.

5. The intensives are formed with reduplication of the second radical: Pôlēl, Pôlal, Hiṯpôlēl. Cf. paradigm.

6. Note the formation of the jussive, and the im-

perfect with wāw consecutive, in Qal and Hipʻîl.

יָקוּם > יָקֹם and וַיָּקָם

יָקִים > יָקֵם and וַיָּקֶם

Hollow verbs ending in laryngeals or ר have patah as the thematic vowel in the jussive and the imperfect with wāw consecutive, e.g., וַיָּסַר 8:13.

Note 1: Observe the conjugation of the stative (verbs whose thematic vowel is either ṣērē or ḥōlem) in the paradigm. מֵתוּ 7:22 יִמּוֹל 17:12 הִמּוֹל 17:10 נָפֹצוּ 10:18 הֵבִיא 4:4 הָאִיר 1:17 מֵקִים 9:9 הֲקִמֹתִי 9:17 וַיָּבֵא 4:3

Note 2: The ע"י is like the ע"ו in all forms except Qal imperfect, imperative, infinitive construct, and passive participle, which retain the yôd.

§57. The Double ע Verb (ע"ע)

The characteristic of these verbs is the doubled second radical. This doubling may be implied, indicated by dāgēš forte, or written fully. The dictionary form is always written fully, e.g., סבב.

1. The stem is monosyllabic except in the Qal infinitive absolute סָבוֹב, the Qal participles סֹבֵב and סָבוּב, and the intensives.

   Note: The secondary forms which are written fully follow the pattern of the strong verb. See paradigm.

2. Whenever afformatives are added to the monosyllabic stem, the second radical must always bear dāgēš forte.

3. Before consonantal afformatives, as in the hollow verbs, a helping vowel is inserted.

   a. In all perfects, except the intensives,

this vowel is ḥōlem (וֹ). It is accented except before תֶּם and תֶּן.

b. In all imperfects and imperatives, except the intensives, this vowel is accented ־ֵי.

4. Vocal afformatives do not draw the accent.

5. The original short vowel of the preformatives of the Qal imperfect, Nip̱ʻal perfect and participle, and all Hip̱ʻîl and Hop̱ʻal forms must be lengthened when it stands in an open unaccented syllable.

6. The monosyllabic stem receives the vowel of the last syllable of the strong verb. Thus Qal perfect (קָטַל) סָבַב becomes סַב; the imperfect (יִקְטֹל) יִסְבֹּב* becomes יָסֹב; the imperative and infinitive construct (קְטֹל) סְבֹב becomes סֹב; the Nip̱ʻal perfect (נִקְטַל) נִסְבַב* becomes נָסַב; the Nip̱ʻal imperfect, imperative, and infinitive construct have paṯaḥ as the ultimate vowel instead of ṣērē, (יִקָּטֵל, הִקָּטֵל, הִקָּטֵל) יִסָּבֵב*, הִסָּבֵב*, הִסָּבֵב* becoming יִסַּב, הִסַּב, הִסַּב; the Hip̱ʻîl has ṣērē as the ultimate vowel instead of ḥîreq yôḏ in an accented syllable, and sometimes has a paṯaḥ (in an unaccented syllable it sometimes has a ḥîreq); the Hop̱ʻal (הָקְטַל etc.) הָסְבַב* becomes הוּסַב.

Note: The intransitive verbs have paṯaḥ as the thematic vowel in the Qal imperfect; the vowel of the preformative in this instance is ṣērē, e.g., אֵקַל 16:5.

7. The intensives may be vocalized like the strong verb or like the hollow verb.

Note: Instead of the second radical being doubled, frequently in the imperfect of Qal, Hip̱ʻîl, and Hop̱ʻal the first radical is doubled. In addition to the expected forms, e.g., יָסֹב, יֵקַל, יָסֵב, יוּסַב, the forms יִסֹּב, יִתַּם, יַסֵּב, יֻסַּב also occur.

§58. The Doubly Weak Verb

Many verbs have more than one weak radical. These verbs usually exhibit the peculiarities characteristic of each weak letter. Observe the following forms:

1. פ"ן and ל"ה:
   - נכה, 'to strike'
     - Hip̱ʿîl perfect הִכָּה, imperfect יַכֶּה, וַיַּךְ, imperative הַכֵּה, הַךְ, infinitives הַכֵּה, הַכּוֹת.
     - Hop̱ʿal הֻכָּה, הֻכֵּיתִי, etc.
     - Nip̱ʿal perfect נִכָּה, etc.
   - נטה, 'to stretch out,' 'to extend'
     - Qal יִטֶּה, וַיֵּט, etc.
2. Other frequent combinations:
   - פ"א and ל"ה: אבה, אפה
   - פ"ו and ל"ה: ידה Hip̱ʿîl perfect הוֹדֵינוּ, etc.
   - פ"ן and ל"א: נשׂא Qal imperfect יִשָּׂא, יִשְׂאוּ; Qal imperative שָׂא, שְׂאוּ; Qal infinitive construct שְׂאֵת, לָשֵׂאת.
   - פ"ו and ל"א: יצא Qal imperfect יֵצֵא, imperative צֵא, infinitive construct צֵאת.

§59. Suggested Helps for the Recognition of Roots

1. When all the radicals of a root appear:
   a. If the vowel of the imperfect preformative is paṯaḥ and the following radical is a strong letter (i.e., not a laryngeal or a vowel letter), the form is Hip̱ʿîl; if the following radical is a laryngeal, the form is either Qal or Hip̱ʿîl.
   b. If a shewa appears under an imperfect preformative, the form will normally be either Piʿēl or Puʿal.
2. When only two radicals of the root appear (only the weak verbs ל"ה, פ"י or פ"ו, ע"ע, hollow, are affected): The following observations ap-

ply to about 90% of such occurrences.

a. When a qāmeṣ (never qāmeṣ ḥāṭûp) occurs in an open preformative, the root will normally be hollow or ע"ע (90% hollow), the form Qal or Hip̱ʿîl.

b. When a ṣērē occurs in an open imperfect preformative, the root will normally be פ"ו, occasionally ל"ה; the form will be Qal.

c. When a ḥîreq occurs in an open imperfect preformative, the root will normally be ל"ה; the form will be Qal.

d. When a paṯaḥ occurs in an open imperfect preformative, the root will normally be ל"ה; if it is followed by a strong radical, the form will be Hip̱ʿîl; if it is followed by a laryngeal, the form will be either Qal or Hip̱ʿîl.

e. When a holem (וֹ) occurs in an open preformative, the root will normally be פ"ו, the form either Nip̱ʿal or Hip̱ʿîl.

f. When neither a preformative nor afformative appears and the vowel of the closed syllable is qāmeṣ, the root is normally hollow.

g. When neither a preformative nor afformative appears and the vowel of the closed syllable is ṣērē, the root is normally פ"ו.

h. When neither a preformative nor afformative appears and the vowel of the closed syllable is paṯaḥ, the root will normally be ע"ע.

Note: When the second of the two radicals is a laryngeal (except א and ה), the vowel tends to be paṯaḥ.

The following table may prove helpful:

Form	Type of Weak Verb
XXָ	Hollow or ע"ע
XXֵ	פ"ו or ל"ה
XXִ	ל"ה
XXַ	ל"ה
XXוֹ	פ"ו (sometimes written defectively ֹ)
XXָ	Hollow
XXֵ	פ"ו
XXַ	ע"ע
The vowel represents the vowel of an open preformative; the X's represent the two remaining radicals.	

The Formation of the Nouns: Nouns appear to have been formed from the verbal root in the following manner:

From the simple root:

§60. With One Original Short Vowel after the First Radical

The vowel was a, i, or u, and accordingly the forms were qaṭl, qiṭl, quṭl. This original monosyllabic form has become disyllabic by the insertion of a helping vowel between the second and third radicals. Because the helping vowel is usually s^{e}gôl this class of nouns is known as segolates. The original vowel which now stands in an open syllable is usually lengthened: pa<u>t</u>aḥ to s^{e}gôl (this s^{e}gôl is a long vowel), ḥîreq to ṣērē, qibbûṣ to ḥōlem.

Regular	Laryngeal פ	Laryngeal ע	Laryngeal ל	ע"ן	ל"ה ל"ו	ל"ה ל"י	Hollow ע"ו	Hollow ע"י	ע"ע
Original short 'a,' qaṭl									
מֶלֶךְ	אֶרֶץ עֶרֶב	נַעַר תַּחַת	זֶרַע	אַף (*אַנְף)	שָׂחוּ	פְּרִי	מָוֶת שׁוֹר	חַיִל זַיִת עַיִן	יָם הַר עַם
Original short 'i,' qiṭl									
סֵפֶר	עֵזֶר עֵצֶב		נֵצַח	עֵז (*עִנְז)		חֲצִי		רִיב	לֵב
Original short 'u,' quṭl									
בֹּקֶר	אֹהֶל חֹשֶׁךְ	פֹּעַל	אֹרַח		תֹּהוּ בֹּהוּ	חֳלִי	גּוּר		חֹק

Note 1: Monosyllabic nouns with an original short vowel after the second radical are rare: e.g., דְּבַשׁ, 'honey,' שְׁכֶם 'shoulder,' בְּאֵר 'well.'

Note 2: The segolates exhibit the following characteristics:

a. The singular construct form of the segolate is usually the same as the absolute.

b. When suffixes are added to the singular segolate, it reverts to the monosyllabic form.

c. The plurals of the segolates take qāmeṣ under the second radical before ים. and וֹת.

d. The vowel in the plural before suffixes is irregular.

e. In pause the penultimate vowel usually reverts to its original vowel and is lengthened, e.g., זֶרַע > זָרַע 1:29.

Note 3: Segolates formed from ע"ע roots appear in the singular as monosyllables (cf. the above table). In the plural and before suffixes the second radical is doubled (on the vowel, cf. §21.1.a.note).

§61. Table of Suffixes to

	king	book	ear	nose	goat
Singular					
Absolute	מֶלֶךְ	סֵפֶר	אֹזֶן	אַף	עֵז
Construct	מֶלֶךְ	סֵפֶר	אֹזֶן	אַף	עֵז
Suffixes					
1 c.s.	מַלְכִּי	סִפְרִי	אָזְנִי	אַפִּי	עִזִּי
2 m.s.	מַלְכְּךָ	סִפְרְךָ	אָזְנְךָ	אַפְּךָ	עִזְּךָ
2 f.s.	מַלְכֵּךְ	סִפְרֵךְ	אָזְנֵךְ	אַפֵּךְ	עִזֵּךְ
3 m.s.	מַלְכּוֹ	סִפְרוֹ	אָזְנוֹ	אַפּוֹ	עִזּוֹ
3 f.s.	מַלְכָּהּ	סִפְרָהּ	אָזְנָהּ	אַפָּהּ	עִזָּהּ
1 c.p.	מַלְכֵּנוּ	סִפְרֵנוּ	אָזְנֵנוּ	אַפֵּנוּ	עִזֵּנוּ
2 m.p.	מַלְכְּכֶם	סִפְרְכֶם	אָזְנְכֶם	אַפְּכֶם	עִזְּכֶם
2 f.p.	מַלְכְּכֶן	סִפְרְכֶן	אָזְנְכֶן	אַפְּכֶן	עִזְּכֶן
3 m.p.	מַלְכָּם	סִפְרָם	אָזְנָם	אַפָּם	עִזָּם
3 f.p.	מַלְכָּן	סִפְרָן	אָזְנָן	אַפָּן	עִזָּן
Plural					
Absolute	מְלָכִים	סְפָרִים	אֳזָנַיִם	אַפַּיִם	עִזִּים
Construct	מַלְכֵי	סִפְרֵי	אָזְנֵי	אַפֵּי	עִזֵּי
Suffixes					
1 c.s.	מְלָכַי	סְפָרַי	אֳזָנַי	אַפַּי	עִזַּי
2 m.s.	מְלָכֶיךָ	סְפָרֶיךָ	אֳזָנֶיךָ	אַפֶּיךָ	עִזֶּיךָ
2 f.s.	מְלָכַיִךְ	סְפָרַיִךְ	אֳזָנַיִךְ	אַפַּיִךְ	עִזַּיִךְ
3 m.s.	מְלָכָיו	סְפָרָיו	אֳזָנָיו	אַפָּיו	עִזָּיו
3 f.s.	מְלָכֶיהָ	סְפָרֶיהָ	אֳזָנֶיהָ	אַפֶּיהָ	עִזֶּיהָ
1 c.p.	מְלָכֵינוּ	סְפָרֵינוּ	אֳזָנֵינוּ	אַפֵּינוּ	עִזֵּינוּ
2 m.p.	מַלְכֵיכֶם	סִפְרֵיכֶם	אָזְנֵיכֶם	אַפֵּיכֶם	עִזֵּיכֶם
2 f.p.	מַלְכֵיכֶן	סִפְרֵיכֶן	אָזְנֵיכֶן	אַפֵּיכֶן	עִזֵּיכֶן
3 m.p.	מַלְכֵיהֶם	סִפְרֵיהֶם	אָזְנֵיהֶם	אַפֵּיהֶם	עִזֵּיהֶם
3 f.p.	מַלְכֵיהֶן	סִפְרֵיהֶן	אָזְנֵיהֶן	אַפֵּיהֶן	עִזֵּיהֶן

Note 1: The total listing of the first five columns does not mean that all the forms occur in the Old Testament; they are listed for the sake of completeness. The last six columns, to the right, represent those forms which occur in the Old Testament.

the qaṭl, qiṭl, quṭl Nouns

Singular						
fruit	death	eye	people	heart	statute	
פְּרִי	מָוֶת	עַיִן	עַם	לֵב	חֹק	Abs.
פְּרִי	מוֹת	עֵין	עַם	לֶב־	חָק־	Const.
						Suffix
פִּרְיִי	מוֹתִי	עֵינִי	עַמִּי	לִבִּי	חֻקִּי	1 c.s.
פִּרְיְךָ		עֵינְךָ	עַמְּךָ	לִבְּךָ	חֻקְּךָ	2 m.s.
				לִבֵּךְ		2 f.s.
פִּרְיוֹ				לִבּוֹ		3 m.s.
				לִבָּהּ		3 f.s.
		עֵינֵנוּ		לִבֵּנוּ		1 c.p.
				לִבְּכֶם		2 m.p.
						2 f.p.
		עֵינָם		לִבָּם		3 m.p.
				לִבָּן		3 f.p.
Plural						
		עֵינַיִם	עַמִּים	לִבּוֹת	חֻקִּים	Abs.
	מוֹתֵי	עֵינֵי	עַמֵּי	לִבּוֹת	חֻקֵּי	Const.
						Suffix
		עֵינַי				1 c.s.
		עֵינֶיךָ				2 m.s.
						2 f.s.
						3 m.s.
						3 f.s.
						1 c.p.
						2 m.p.
						2 f.p.
						3 m.p.
						3 f.p.

Note 2: The infinitives construct of the פ"ו verbs and some of the פ"ן verbs are segolates. They take their suffixes according to one of these columns, depending on their original vowels. The infinitive construct of נתן, 'to give,' takes its suffixes on the analogy of עֵץ.

§62. With Two Original Short Vowels

a-a qaṭal (a-a > ā-ā)						
Regular	Laryngeal פ	ע	ל	ל"י or ל"ו	Hollow	ע"ע
דָּבָר	אָשָׁם	רָעָב	שָׂבָע	שָׂדֶה הָרֶה שָׂדַי[1] עָנָו	רָם טוֹב	עָנָן חָלָל
a-i qaṭil (a-i > ā-ē)						
זָקֵן כָּבֵד	עָקֵב	בְּהֵמָה		עָנִי	מֵת	
a-u qaṭul (a-u > ā-ō)						
קָטֹן נָקֹד	אָדֹם	Note: The final consonant is doubled before afformatives of gender and number to preserve the original short 'u.' נְקֻדִּים 30:39.				
i-a qiṭal (i-a > ē-ā)						
שֵׁבָר	צֵלָע			רֵעַ רֵעֶה		לֵבָב

[1]Original ל"י is almost always rejected and its vowel becomes ◌ֶה. In construct this ◌ֶה always becomes ◌ֵה.

§63. With One Long Vowel after the First Radical

Original long 'a'(â)-a qâṭal (â-a > ô-ā)		
Regular	Laryngeal	ל"ה
	עוֹלָם	רֹאֶה Note: Long 'a'(â) is normally changed to ḥōlem in Hebrew. Nouns ending in ◌ֶה always become ◌ֵה in construct.
Original long 'a'(â)-i qâṭil (â-i > ô-ē)		
קֹטֵל	כֹּהֵן	
Original long 'u'(û)-a qûṭal (û-a > û-ā)		
	עוּגָב	

Table of Suffixes to Illustrate §§ 62-64

Singular					
	word	old	eternity	seer	peace
Absolute	דָּבָר	זָקֵן	עוֹלָם	רֹאֶה	שָׁלוֹם
Construct	דְּבַר	זְקַן	עוֹלַם	רֹאֵה	שְׁלוֹם
Suffixes					
1 c.s.	דְּבָרִי	זְקֵנִי	עוֹלָמִי	רֹאִי	שְׁלוֹמִי
2 m.s.	דְּבָרְךָ	זְקֶנְךָ	עוֹלָמְךָ	רֹאֲךָ	שְׁלוֹמְךָ
2 f.s.	דְּבָרֵךְ	זְקֵנֵךְ	עוֹלָמֵךְ	רֹאֵךְ	שְׁלוֹמֵךְ
3 m.s.	דְּבָרוֹ	זְקֵנוֹ	עוֹלָמוֹ	רֹאוֹ	שְׁלוֹמוֹ
3 f.s.	דְּבָרָהּ	זְקֵנָהּ	עוֹלָמָהּ	רֹאָהּ	שְׁלוֹמָהּ
1 c.p.	דְּבָרֵנוּ	זְקֵנֵנוּ	עוֹלָמֵנוּ	רֹאֵנוּ	שְׁלוֹמֵנוּ
2 m.p.	דְּבַרְכֶם	זְקֶנְכֶם	עוֹלַמְכֶם	רֹאֲכֶם	שְׁלוֹמְכֶם
2 f.p.	דְּבַרְכֶן	זְקֶנְכֶן	עוֹלַמְכֶן	רֹאֲכֶן	שְׁלוֹמְכֶן
3 m.p.	דְּבָרָם	זְקֵנָם	עוֹלָמָם	רֹאָם	שְׁלוֹמָם
3 f.p.	דְּבָרָן	זְקֵנָן	עוֹלָמָן	רֹאָן	שְׁלוֹמָן
Plural					
Absolute	דְּבָרִים	זְקֵנִים	עוֹלָמִים	רֹאִים	שְׁלוֹמִים
Construct	דִּבְרֵי	זִקְנֵי	עוֹלְמֵי	רֹאֵי	שְׁלוֹמֵי
Suffixes					
1 c.s.	דְּבָרַי	זְקֵנַי	עוֹלָמַי	רֹאַי	שְׁלוֹמַי
2 m.s.	דְּבָרֶיךָ	זְקֵנֶיךָ	עוֹלָמֶיךָ	רֹאֶיךָ	שְׁלוֹמֶיךָ
2 f.s.	דְּבָרַיִךְ	זְקֵנַיִךְ	עוֹלָמַיִךְ	רֹאַיִךְ	שְׁלוֹמַיִךְ
3 m.s.	דְּבָרָיו	זְקֵנָיו	עוֹלָמָיו	רֹאָיו	שְׁלוֹמָיו
3 f.s.	דְּבָרֶיהָ	זְקֵנֶיהָ	עוֹלָמֶיהָ	רֹאֶיהָ	שְׁלוֹמֶיהָ
1 c.p.	דְּבָרֵינוּ	זְקֵנֵינוּ	עוֹלָמֵינוּ	רֹאֵינוּ	שְׁלוֹמֵינוּ
2 m.p.	דִּבְרֵיכֶם	זִקְנֵיכֶם	עוֹלְמֵיכֶם	רֹאֵיכֶם	שְׁלוֹמֵיכֶם
2 f.p.	דִּבְרֵיכֶן	זִקְנֵיכֶן	עוֹלְמֵיכֶן	רֹאֵיכֶן	שְׁלוֹמֵיכֶן
3 m.p.	דִּבְרֵיהֶם	זִקְנֵיהֶם	עוֹלְמֵיהֶם	רֹאֵיהֶם	שְׁלוֹמֵיהֶם
3 f.p.	דִּבְרֵיהֶן	זִקְנֵיהֶן	עוֹלְמֵיהֶן	רֹאֵיהֶן	שְׁלוֹמֵיהֶן

Note: Any noun ending in ֶה will take suffixes on the analogy of רֹאֶה, i.e., the final vowel is dropped before suffixes.

§64. <u>With One Long Vowel after the Second Radical</u>

a-â qaṭâl (a-â > ā-ô)	a-î qaṭîl (a-î > ā-î)	a-û qaṭûl (a-û > ā-û)
קָדוֹשׁ גָּדוֹל שָׁלוֹם	עָנִי מָשִׁיחַ נָבִיא	אָרוּר עָרוּם
qᵉṭâl	qᵉṭîl	qᵉṭûl
שְׁאָר אֱנוֹשׁ חֲמוֹר	פְּסִיל חֲזִיר	רְכוּשׁ גְּדוּל אֱמוּנָה

§65. <u>From the Intensive Stems</u>

Second radical doubled	Third radical reduplicated	Two radicals reduplicated
שַׁבָּת אִלֵּם יַבָּשָׁה עִוֵּר חָרָבָה חֵרֵשׁ חַטָּאָה גִּבּוֹר צַדִּיק	שַׁאֲנָן רַעֲנָן	גִּלְגַּל

§66. <u>With the Addition of a Preformative</u>

1. Preformative מ:
   a. Of place מָקוֹם, מִזְבֵּחַ, מִשְׁכָּן, מוֹשָׁב, מַמְלָכָה, מִדְבָּר.
   b. Of instrument מַאֲכֶלֶת, מִפְתֵּחַ.
   Note: A large number of nouns with prefixed מ does not fit the above categories.
2. Preformative ת (mostly feminine):
   תּוֹלֶדֶת, תַּרְדֵּמָה, תְּשׁוּקָה, תְּפִלָּה, תּוֹרָה, תְּאֵנָה, תְּהוֹם.
3. Other preformatives of less frequent occurrence are א and ה. אֶצְבַּע, הַצָּלָה (נצל)

§67. With the Addition of an Afformative

1. Nouns are sometimes formed by the addition of ל, ם, ן.
2. The afformative ִי usually indicates origin, thus:

   רַגְלִי 'a footman' (infantry man)

   עִבְרִי 'a Hebrew' (one belonging to the tribe of עבר)

   שִׁשִּׁי 'a sixth' (belonging to the class of six)

   The feminine ending is ִיָּה or ִית, thus:

   m. מוֹאָבִי 'a Moabite'

   f. מוֹאֲבִיָּה or מוֹאֲבִית 'a Moabitess'
3. וּת (sometimes ִית) is added to concrete nouns to form abstractions:

   רֵאשִׁית 'beginning'

   מַלְכוּת 'kingdom'

§68. Some Characteristics of Feminine Nouns

1. Segolates form their feminines by adding ָה to the monosyllabic stem.

   מַלְכָּה, נַעֲרָה, חֶרְפָּה

   Note: The suffixes are added throughout to the plural by adding them to the construct form.
2. Feminine nouns ending in ֶת:

   a. These are treated as segolates. Cf. §39.5.

   b. The singular absolute and construct forms are alike.

Note: Names of

elements (earth, stone, etc.),

organs of the body appearing in pairs (hand, eye, etc.),

utensils (sword, cup, etc.),

are usually feminine.

§69. <u>The Numerals</u>

	Cardinals				Ordinals
	With masculine nouns		With feminine nouns		
	Abs.	Const.	Abs.	Const.	
1	אֶחָד	אַחַד	אַחַת	אַחַת	רִאשׁוֹן
2	שְׁנַיִם	שְׁנֵי	שְׁתַּיִם	שְׁתֵּי	שֵׁנִי
3	שְׁלֹשָׁה	שְׁלֹשֶׁת	שָׁלֹשׁ	שְׁלֹשׁ	שְׁלִישִׁי
4	אַרְבָּעָה	אַרְבַּעַת	אַרְבַּע	אַרְבַּע	רְבִיעִי
5	חֲמִשָּׁה	חֲמֵשֶׁת	חָמֵשׁ	חֲמֵשׁ	(חֲמִשִׁי) חֲמִישִׁי
6	שִׁשָּׁה	שֵׁשֶׁת	שֵׁשׁ	שֵׁשׁ	שִׁשִּׁי
7	שִׁבְעָה	שִׁבְעַת	שֶׁבַע	שְׁבַע	שְׁבִיעִי
8	שְׁמֹנָה	שְׁמֹנַת	שְׁמֹנֶה	שְׁמֹנֶה	שְׁמִינִי
9	תִּשְׁעָה	תִּשְׁעַת	תֵּשַׁע	תְּשַׁע	תְּשִׁיעִי
10	עֲשָׂרָה	עֲשֶׂרֶת	עֶשֶׂר	עֶשֶׂר	עֲשִׂירִי

1. The numerals 3-10 are nouns having the peculiarity that when they occur with masculine nouns they take a feminine form; when they occur with feminine nouns they take a masculine form. The explanation of this phenomenon is uncertain.
2. The numerals 2-10 may be connected with their noun in one of three ways:
   a. In the construct state before the noun.
   b. In the absolute state before the noun.
   c. In the absolute state after the noun.
3. The numeral אֶחָד is an adjective; the numeral שְׁנַיִם or שְׁתַּיִם is a noun.
4. The numerals 11-19 are formed by adding the numeral 10 to the units as two independent words without a connecting wāw. Note the secondary forms for 11 and 12 and the secondary form for 10 which never occurs alone. Certain nouns, frequently used with numerals, e.g., יוֹם, שָׁנָה, אִישׁ, נֶפֶשׁ, etc., occur in the singular after the numerals 11-19.

	With masculine nouns	With feminine nouns
11	עַשְׁתֵּי עָשָׂר, אַחַד עָשָׂר	עַשְׁתֵּי עֶשְׂרֵה, אַחַת עֶשְׂרֵה
12	שְׁנֵים עָשָׂר, שְׁנֵי עָשָׂר	שְׁתֵּים עֶשְׂרֵה, שְׁתֵּי עֶשְׂרֵה
13	שְׁלֹשָׁה עָשָׂר	שְׁלֹשׁ עֶשְׂרֵה
14	אַרְבָּעָה עָשָׂר	אַרְבַּע עֶשְׂרֵה
15	חֲמִשָּׁה עָשָׂר	חֲמֵשׁ עֶשְׂרֵה

5. The tens (30, 40, 50, 60, etc.) are formed by adding the masculine plural afformative ִים to the corresponding units (3-9), except 20, which is the plural of 10. These are indeclinable. The units are joined to the tens with waw; the units may either precede or follow the tens.

20. עֶשְׂרִים　　21. אֶחָד וְעֶשְׂרִים
30. שְׁלֹשִׁים
40. אַרְבָּעִים
50. חֲמִשִּׁים
60. שִׁשִּׁים
70. שִׁבְעִים
80. שְׁמֹנִים
90. תִּשְׁעִים

The numbered object follows in the singular, precedes in the plural.

6. The hundreds stand before the numbered object in the absolute or construct.

100. מֵאָה אַחַת　　1000. אֶלֶף אֶחָד
200. שְׁתֵּי מֵאוֹת　　2000. שְׁנֵי אֲלָפִים
300. שְׁלֹשׁ מֵאוֹת　　10,000. עֲשֶׂרֶת אֲלָפִים; רְבָבָה
400. אַרְבַּע מֵאוֹת
500. חֲמֵשׁ מֵאוֹת
600. שֵׁשׁ מֵאוֹת
700. שְׁבַע מֵאוֹת
800. שְׁמֹנֶה מֵאוֹת
900. תְּשַׁע מֵאוֹת

7. The ordinals, except רִאשׁוֹן 'first,' are formed from the corresponding cardinals by adding hireq yôd̲ at the end and between the second and third radicals. Cf. table, p. 86.

8. The feminine of the ordinal is used to express fractions. Multiples may be expressed by the dual or by פַּעַם. The distributive is expressed by repetition of the cardinal. שִׁבְעָה שִׁבְעָה, 'seven pairs' 7:2; שְׁנַיִם שְׁנַיִם 'two by two' 7:9.

9. The consonants have the following numerical equivalents:

א = 1	יא = 11	י = 10
ב = 2	יב = 12	ך = 20
ג = 3	יג = 13	ל = 30
ד = 4	יד = 14	ם = 40
ה = 5	טו = 15	ן = 50
ו = 6	טז = 16	ס = 60
ז = 7	יז = 17	ע = 70
ח = 8	יח = 18	ף = 80
ט = 9	יט = 19	ץ = 90
י =10	ך = 20	ק =100
		ר =200
		ש =300
		ת =400

PART III

§70. The Uses of Prepositions

1. בְּ - 'in,' 'on,' 'with,' 'by'

The preposition בְּ is generally the Hebrew equivalent of the Latin 'in,' the Greek 'ἐν,' denoting place of rest.

'in' Gen. 1:1,6,14

'on' Gen. 8:20

'by' 1 Sam. 29:1

'with' Gen. 32:11

a. It may often be translated:

1) 'among' (consisting in or of) Gen. 7:21

2) 'as' (in the essence of) Ex. 6:3

3) 'of' (share in) Ex. 12:3

4) 'against' (with hostility toward) Gen. 16:12

b. It is often left untranslated with certain transitive verbs which denote:

1) Contact:

נגע 'touch,' נכה 'strike,' אחז 'seize,' ראה 'see,' שׁמע 'hear,' קרא 'call,' שׁאל 'ask'

2) Authority:

מלך, מֹשל, נגשׂ, רדה 'to rule,' i.e., 'to have dominion over'

c. It may be used to denote instrument ('with') or price ('for'). Gen. 30:16; Josh. 10:11.

d. It may be used in connection with an infinitive construct to introduce a temporal phrase. Gen. 2:4 בְּהִבָּרְאָם "in the creating of them," i.e., "when they were created." Cf. also Gen. 4:8.

2. לְ - 'to,' 'into,' 'for,' 'at,' 'with reference to'

The preposition לְ generally expresses direction toward either in a physical or temporal sense (for the latter, cf. Ex. 34:25).

'in' Gen. 1:29

'into' Gen. 2:22

'for' Gen. 24:4

'at' Gen. 4:7

'with reference to' Gen. 17:10

a. It is often used with the infinitive construct:

1) To denote purpose. Gen. 1:15, 11:5, 28:4.

2) With היה

a) To denote continuing action (i.e., 'in the act of,' 'ready to'). Gen. 15:12.

b) To denote compulsion. Josh. 2:5.

3) When the infinitive is construed as the direct object of the verb. Gen. 4:2, 12:11.

Note: The regular negative before the infinitive construct is לְבִלְתִּי. Gen. 3:11, 4:15.

b. It is sometimes used to introduce a direct object. Gen. 9:27.

c. It is often used to circumvent the construct relation. Since the two members of a construct relation must agree in definiteness (e.g., '<u>the</u> house of <u>the</u> man'), whenever a definite noun is closely related to an indefinite noun (e.g., 'the house of a man,' 'a house of the man') the preposition לְ is necessary. Gen. 7:11, 20:18.

d. It is normally prefixed to the agent with a

passive verb. Gen. 25:21.

e. It is frequently used after imperatives to emphasize the subject. Gen. 12:1, 22:2.

f. When it is prefixed to פְּנֵי, עֵינֵי, מַעַן, פִּי, the meaning of these nouns is subordinated to the prepositional idea, e.g., לִפְנֵי, לְעֵינֵי 'before'; לְמַעַן 'because of,' 'for the sake of,' 'so that'; לְפִי 'in accordance with.'

3. כְּ - 'as,' 'like,' 'according to,' 'approximately'

The preposition כְּ generally expresses identity or similarity.

'like,' 'as' Gen. 13:10

'according to' Gen. 1:26, 4:17

a. It often expresses approximation before words of number, mass, or time.

'even' Gen. 25:31

'about' Ruth 1:4, Num. 11:31

b. It may express agreement.

'in accordance with' 2 Kings 1:17

c. It may be used correlatively.

'like . . . so' Num. 2:17, Lev. 7:7

'the more . . . the more' Ex. 1:12

d. It often combines with מוֹ. Cf. §38.

e. When it is prefixed to פִּי it means 'commensurate with.' Ex. 16:21

4. מִן - 'out of,' 'from,' 'away from'

The preposition מִן normally expresses the idea of separation.

'from' Gen. 1:7, 2:2, 22:12

'away from' Gen. 4:11, 2:8, 12:8

a. It may often be translated:

1) 'from among' Gen. 3:1

2) 'without' (from a lack of)

3) 'from being,' 'from doing' Gen. 16:2

(usually after verbs denoting restraint or refusal; the idea of negation is denoted after other verbs)

4) 'because,' 'on account of'

5) 'some' (partitive use) Ex. 16:27, Gen. 19:32.

b. It is used to express the comparative. Gen. 29:19, 26:16. It is used to express comparison after an adjective which in English is in the comparative degree.

c. It may combine with פְּנֵי with the meaning 'because of.' Gen. 41:31.

5. עַל - 'upon,' 'concerning,' 'over'

The preposition עַל usually expresses the idea 'upon,' 'over.'

'upon' Gen. 1:2

'concerning' Gen. 41:15

'over' Gen. 1:20

'at,' 'beside' Gen. 16:7, 18:8

Note: The preposition still retains its original meaning 'over' in the sense of pre-eminence, elevation.

a. It may be translated:

1) 'because' (introducing causal clauses) Gen. 20:3

2) 'although' (introducing concessive clauses)

3) 'against' Gen. 34:25,27

b. When it follows verbs of command, it may be left untranslated.

6. The following are commonly used prepositions:

אַחֵר 'another'

אַחֲרֵי 'after'

אֶל 'at,' 'to,' 'toward' (a place or person)

Note: Late writers under the influence of Aramaic often used אֶל and עַל

interchangeably.

אֵצֶל	'by,' 'near,' 'beside'
אֵת	'with'
בִּגְלַל	'on account of'
בֵּין	'between'
בַּעֲבוּר	'for the sake of'
בְּעַד	'for the sake of,' 'in behalf of,' 'through'
זוּלַת	'besides'
יַעַן	'because of'
לְמַעַן	'because of'
לִפְנֵי	'before
נֶגֶד	'opposite'
עַד	'unto,' 'until (a place or person)'
עִם	'with,' 'by,' 'against'
תַּחַת	'under,' 'instead of'

§71. <u>The Infinitive</u>

The Hebrew infinitive is a verbal noun and may function either as a verb or as a noun. Like the participle it is timeless, i.e., it may express present, past, or future time, depending on the context. The infinitive takes two forms.

1. The Infinitive Absolute
   - a. The infinitive absolute may neither govern a genitive nor be governed by a preceding preposition.
   - b. It may stand independently as a finite verb and thus may take an object in the accusative. The form (perfect, imperfect, imperative) of the finite verb which the infinitive absolute then represents must be determined from the context.
   - c. It may be used as the object of a finite verb (with nominal or adverbial force).
     - 1) With verbs of the same root:
       - a) It may immediately precede the

verb to strengthen the verbal idea, e.g., מוֹת תָּמוּת, literally 'dying, you shall die,' i.e., 'you shall surely die.' Gen. 2:17.

b) It may follow the verb to indicate continuation of the verbal idea.

2) With verbs of different roots, it may be used to define the verbal idea more closely. Josh. 11:11.

Note: The infinitive absolute indicating continuation of the verbal idea may be followed or preceded by a second infinitive absolute of a different root. Gen. 8:3.

d. It may be used as the subject or predicate nominative of a sentence. Prov. 25:27.

2. The Infinitive Construct

a. The infinitive construct may function as subject of the sentence, object of a preposition, or object of the verb. Gen. 2:18 (subj.), 2:17 (obj. of prep.), 21:6 (obj.).

b. It may appear as the first member of a construct relation. In this usage the second member of the construct relation may be either subject or object of the infinitive (cf. §39.4.d). Gen. 2:4. The context must determine whether the second member is subject or object.

§72. The Participle

1. When used as a noun the participle follows the syntax of the noun.
2. When used as an adjective the participle is subject to the rules of the adjective. Cf. §41.

3. When used as a verb:
   a. The participle is normally preceded by an expressed subject with which it agrees in number and gender. Gen. 1:2. It may be introduced by כִּי. Gen. 3:5.
   b. The participle may take an object. Gen. 1:11.
   c. The participle is timeless, i.e., the context must determine whether it refers to present, past, or future time.

§73. The Sentence

Every Hebrew sentence is either nominal or verbal. The nominal sentence emphasizes some characteristic of the subject; the verbal sentence stresses the act or condition of the subject. In the nominal sentence both subject and predicate are substantives (noun, adjective, adverb, prepositional phrase, or pronoun suffix joined to a participle). In the verbal sentence the predicate is a finite verb. The verbal sentence is the more common method of expression. The verb היה may either be used as a copula in a nominal sentence, or it may retain its full verbal force in the sense of 'to become,' 'to happen,' 'to exist' in a verbal sentence.

1. The Simple Declarative Sentence
   a. The normal word order in the nominal sentence is subject-predicate. The predicate may precede, however, if it specifically is stressed, e.g., מֵחָרָן אֲנָחְנוּ Gen. 29:4, "We are from Ḥaran!"
   b. The normal word order in the verbal sentence is verb-subject. The subject may precede, however, if it specifically is stressed.
   c. The nominal sentence is ordinarily negated

by לֹא. It is often negated also by אַיִן.

d. Subject of the verbal sentence:

1) The indefinite subject is expressed:

a) Usually by the 3 m.p. of the verb.

b) Often by the 3 m.s. of the verb.

c) In geographical references by the 2 m.s.

d) By the passive. Gen. 4:26.

2) The impersonal subject (Eng. 'it') is usually expressed by the 3 m.s. (Gen. 4:6); occasionally by 3 f.s.

e. Subject and predicate always agree in number and gender, unless the predicate precedes the subject or is a collective noun.

2. The Complex Sentence

a. The relative sentence is normally introduced by אֲשֶׁר (§45); sometimes, especially in poetry, by זֶה, זוּ, זוֹ. Frequently in poetry the relative particle is not expressed; so also in prose after an indefinite antecedent. Gen. 15:13.

1) The relative pronoun in English may be subject of a verb, object of a verb or preposition, or possessive relative. E.g.,

'the man who comes . . .'
'the man whom I saw . . .'
'the house in which I lived . . .'
'the nation whose king is the Lord'

In Hebrew as a rule the relative pronoun is simply a connecting link and usually requires a following supplementary pronoun, or an adverb of direction (e.g., שָׁם), to define more closely the relationship of אֲשֶׁר to its antecedent.

a) The relative as subject:
'Every creeping thing which is living . . .' Gen. 9:3.

b) The relative as object of the verb:
'The prophet whom Yahweh hath sent . . .' Jer. 28:9.

c) The relative as object of a preposition:
'In which is its seed . . .' ('whose seed is in it') Gen. 1:11.

d) The relative with an adverb of direction: Gen. 2:11, 3:23, 20:13.

2) The relative pronoun אֲשֶׁר often does not require a following supplementary pronoun to define closely its relationship to its antecedent:

a) The relative as subject: Gen. 1:7.

b) The relative as object of the verb: Gen. 14:24, 1:21, 2:8.

c) The relative as object of a preposition: Gen. 35:13.

Note: 'in which' אֲשֶׁר...בוֹ Gen. 1:11
'where,' 'whence' אֲשֶׁר...שָׁם
'he who' אֲשֶׁר
'him who' אֵת אֲשֶׁר
'to him who' לַאֲשֶׁר

b. The conditional sentence is normally introduced by אִם, לוּ, or כִּי (אִם expresses a simple condition; the condition introduced by לוּ is not true and cannot be fulfilled). Conditions often must be determined from the context in the absence of an introductory particle.

Note: For other types of clauses, which may normally be recognized in their context, cf. Gesenius-Kautzsch, §§ 155-166.

3. Special Types of Sentences

a. The negative sentence may be introduced by any one of the following particles:

1) לֹא, the normal negative for perfect and imperfect (corresponds to Greek οὐ). It may not stand before a participle, infinitive absolute, or infinitive construct.

2) אַל, the normal negative with jussive and cohortative (corresponds to Greek μή).

3) טֶרֶם, 'not yet,' usually with the imperfect. Gen. 2:5.

4) אַיִן, אֵין, 'nothing,' 'there is not' (implying non-existence). This is the negative of יֵשׁ, 'there is.' This negative normally occurs with a noun, participle, or pronoun.

5) בִּלְתִּי, לְבִלְתִּי, the normal negative with the infinitive construct. Gen. 3:11, 4:15.

6) אֶפֶס, 'no longer,' poetic synonym of אַיִן.

7) בְּלִי, בַּל, poetic synonyms for לֹא.

Note: פֶּן־, 'lest,' normally introduces the negative clause.

b. The interrogative sentence which may be answered 'yes' or 'no' is normally introduced by הֲ; cf. §44. The interrogative particle אִם is used to introduce the second member of a double interrogative sentence. Gen. 37:8,32.

c. The oath is expressed by a conditional sentence introduced by אִם, 'assuredly not,' or אִם לוֹ, 'assuredly,' in which the apodosis has been dropped and must be understood.

§74. <u>Further Observations on Hebrew Vowels</u> (Cf. §§ 5, 21)

1. The original Hebrew vowels were a, i, u, which occurred either as long or short. The long vowels a, i, u have remained unchangeable. In addition to the original long vowels, other long vowels have arisen through compensatory lengthening (cf., e.g., §13.1.a) or the contraction of a diphthong consisting of a short vowel and a following wāw or yôd. For example:

i + y = î (ִי)	יִיטַב from *יִיְטַב	Cf. also §17.2.note.
a + y = ê (ֵי)	עֵין, עַיִן	
a + y = e(y) (ֶי)	תִּגְלֶינָה	
a + w = ô (וֹ)	יוֹצֵא from *יַוְצֵא	
u + w = û (וּ)	יוּצָא from *יֻוְצָא	

Note: When ay is final the y becomes ה.

תִּגְלֶה < תִּגְלַי*

2. The diphthong which is not contracted is rare in Hebrew (חַי 'life,' גּוֹי 'nation,' גָּלוּי). The combination within a word of a short a or i with a following yôd or wāw, e.g., בַּיִת, מָוֶת, apparently represents an original diphthong, which instead of having been contracted has received a helping vowel (cf. §60, the segolates). When the diphthong, however, loses its accent (in the construct state) contraction (cf. 1 above) occurs.

3. The original quantity of the Hebrew vowels is often difficult to determine. The lengths of the vowels may be approximately determined by the following table (cf. §§ 3, 4):

â - original long
ā - derived long
a - original short

ê - derived long
ē - derived long
e - original long, derived long, original short

î - original long
i - original short

ô - original long (a to o shift) or derived long
ō - derived long
o - derived short

u - original short
û - (original long; rarely occurs)

4. Some vowels represent different original vowels:

â is original

ā is derived either from an accented a or an a in a near open syllable (דָּבָר)

a is usually original; sometimes it represents an original i (בַּת)

ê is derived from ay (בֵּין)

ē is derived either from an accented i or an i in a near open syllable

e is derived either from a, i, or ay (אֶרֶץ, שָׂדֶה ,נֶחְמָד)

î is original unless derived from iy (î is almost always written ִי)

i is often original, often derived from a (אִמִּי, יִקְטֹל)

ô is derived from â or aw (שָׁלוֹם, יוֹם)

ō is derived either from an accented o, u or an o, u in a near open syllable (גּוֹאֵל, חֹשֶׁךְ)

o is derived from u (אָכְלָה)

u is original (חֻקִּים)

5. The changes from the original vowels to Biblical Hebrew vowels may be understood from the following rules:

a. In a closed syllable the original vowel is short; it changes according to the table:

	Class of vowel		
	a	i	u
Accented	a verb ā noun	ē	ō
Unaccented	i or a	i or a e with laryngeals	o u in sharpened syllable

b. In an open syllable the original vowel is long or short. The originally long remains long; the originally short is normally lengthened or reduced to shewa (cf. §21).

§75. K^{e}ṯîḇ and Q^{e}rē’

1. The terms k^{e}ṯîḇ and q^{e}rē’ are Aramaic passive participles meaning (what is) 'written' and (what is to be) 'read.' The k^{e}ṯîḇ refers to the word actually written in the text of the Hebrew Bible; the q^{e}rē’ is the variant marginal reading, which according to the Masoretes should be substituted for the k^{e}ṯîḇ. There are cases, however, where the k^{e}ṯîḇ seems to be preferable.

2. Some words are always to be read otherwise than according to k^{e}ṯîḇ. Since these words are easily recognized, the marginal variant q^{e}rē’ is generally omitted and the vowel points of q^{e}rē’ are written under the consonants of the k^{e}ṯîḇ in the text. This combination of conso-

nantal k^eṯîḇ and vocalic q^erē' is called q^erē' perpetuum. An example of this is the divine name: K יְהוָה (Q אֲדֹנָי) or יֱהוִה (Q אֱלֹהִים).

§76. The Accents

The accents were introduced in §12. The following are some of the important disjunctive and conjunctive accents. They are listed more or less in the order of importance.

1. Disjunctive Accents:

- בֽ Sillûq
- ב֑ 'Aṯnāḥ
- ב֫ '‘Ôle(h) w^eyôrēḏ (found in poetry, where it is a stronger divider than the 'Aṯnāḥ)
- ב֔ Zāqēp̱ qāṭôn
- ב֕ Zāqēp̱ gāḏôl
- ב֒ S^eḡôltā'
- ב֗ R^eḇî(a)‘
- ב֓ Šalšeleṯ
- ב֖ Ṭip̱ḥā'
- ב֮ Zarqā'
- ב֙ Pašṭā'
- ב֚ Y^eṯîḇ
- ב֡ Pāzēr
- ב֠ T^elîšā' g^eḏôlâ
- ב֜ Gereš
- ב֞ G^erašayim
- ב֣ | L^eḡarmeh
- ב֟ Pāzēr gāḏôl

2. Conjunctive Accents:

- ב֣ Mûnaḥ
- ב֥ Mêr^{e}ḵā'
- ב֤ Mahpāḵ
- ב֧ Dargā'
- ב֨ 'Azlā'
- ב֩ T^elîšā'

For further reference consult Gesenius-Kautzsch, §15.

PARADIGMS AND HELPS

	Qal	Nip'al	Pi'ēl	Pu'al
Perfect				
3 m.s.	קָטַל	נִקְטַל	קִטֵּל	קֻטַּל
3 f.s.	קָֽטְלָה	נִקְטְלָה	קִטְּלָה	קֻטְּלָה
2 m.s.	קָטַלְתָּ	נִקְטַלְתָּ	קִטַּלְתָּ	קֻטַּלְתָּ
2 f.s.	קָטַלְתְּ	נִקְטַלְתְּ	קִטַּלְתְּ	קֻטַּלְתְּ
1 c.s.	קָטַלְתִּי	נִקְטַלְתִּי	קִטַּלְתִּי	קֻטַּלְתִּי
3 c.p.	קָֽטְלוּ	נִקְטְלוּ	קִטְּלוּ	קֻטְּלוּ
2 m.p.	קְטַלְתֶּם	נִקְטַלְתֶּם	קִטַּלְתֶּם	קֻטַּלְתֶּם
2 f.p.	קְטַלְתֶּן	נִקְטַלְתֶּן	קִטַּלְתֶּן	קֻטַּלְתֶּן
1 c.p.	קָטַלְנוּ	נִקְטַלְנוּ	קִטַּלְנוּ	קֻטַּלְנוּ
Imperfect				
3 m.s.	יִקְטֹל	יִקָּטֵל	יְקַטֵּל	יְקֻטַּל
3 f.s.	תִּקְטֹל	תִּקָּטֵל	תְּקַטֵּל	תְּקֻטַּל
2 m.s.	תִּקְטֹל	תִּקָּטֵל	תְּקַטֵּל	תְּקֻטַּל
2 f.s.	תִּקְטְלִי	תִּקָּטְלִי	תְּקַטְּלִי	תְּקֻטְּלִי
1 c.s.	אֶקְטֹל	אֶקָּטֵל	אֲקַטֵּל	אֲקֻטַּל
3 m.p.	יִקְטְלוּ	יִקָּטְלוּ	יְקַטְּלוּ	יְקֻטְּלוּ
3 f.p.	תִּקְטֹלְנָה	תִּקָּטַלְנָה	תְּקַטֵּלְנָה	תְּקֻטַּלְנָה
2 m.p.	תִּקְטְלוּ	תִּקָּטְלוּ	תְּקַטְּלוּ	תְּקֻטְּלוּ
2 f.p.	תִּקְטֹלְנָה	תִּקָּטַלְנָה	תְּקַטֵּלְנָה	תְּקֻטַּלְנָה
1 c.p.	נִקְטֹל	נִקָּטֵל	נְקַטֵּל	נְקֻטַּל
Imperative				
2 m.s.	קְטֹל	הִקָּטֵל	קַטֵּל	
2 f.s.	קִטְלִי	הִקָּטְלִי	קַטְּלִי	
2 m.p.	קִטְלוּ	הִקָּטְלוּ	קַטְּלוּ	
2 f.p.	קְטֹלְנָה	הִקָּטַלְנָה	קַטֵּלְנָה	
Infinitive				
Absolute	קָטוֹל	הִקָּטֹל נִקְטֹל	קַטֹּל	קֻטֹּל
Construct	קְטֹל	הִקָּטֵל	קַטֵּל	קֻטַּל
Participle				
Active	קֹטֵל		מְקַטֵּל	
Passive	קָטוּל	נִקְטָל		מְקֻטָּל
Imperfect ו consecut.	וַיִּקְטֹל	וַיִּקָּטֵל	וַיְקַטֵּל	וַיְקֻטַּל
Jussive	יִקְטֹל	יִקָּטֵל	יְקַטֵּל	יְקֻטַּל
Cohortative	אֶקְטְלָה	אֶקָּטְלָה	אֲקַטְּלָה	

Refer to §§ 22-32.

Hitpa'ēl	Hip'îl	Hop'al	Stative Qal	
הִתְקַטֵּל	הִקְטִיל	הָקְטַל	כָּבֵד	קָטֹן
הִתְקַטְּלָה	הִקְטִ֫ילָה	הָקְטְלָה	כָּֽבְדָה	קָֽטְנָה
הִתְקַטַּ֫לְתָּ	הִקְטַ֫לְתָּ	הָקְטַ֫לְתָּ	כָּבַ֫דְתָּ	קָטֹ֫נְתָּ
הִתְקַטַּלְתְּ	הִקְטַלְתְּ	הָקְטַלְתְּ	כָּבַדְתְּ	קָטֹנְתְּ
הִתְקַטַּ֫לְתִּי	הִקְטַ֫לְתִּי	הָקְטַ֫לְתִּי	כָּבַ֫דְתִּי	קָטֹ֫נְתִּי
הִתְקַטְּלוּ	הִקְטִ֫ילוּ	הָקְטְלוּ	כָּֽבְדוּ	קָֽטְנוּ
הִתְקַטַּלְתֶּם	הִקְטַלְתֶּם	הָקְטַלְתֶּם	כְּבַדְתֶּם	קְטָנְתֶּם
הִתְקַטַּלְתֶּן	הִקְטַלְתֶּן	הָקְטַלְתֶּן	כְּבַדְתֶּן	קְטָנְתֶּן
הִתְקַטַּ֫לְנוּ	הִקְטַ֫לְנוּ	הָקְטַ֫לְנוּ	כָּבַ֫דְנוּ	קָטֹ֫נּוּ
יִתְקַטֵּל	יַקְטִיל	יָקְטַל	יִכְבַּד	יִקְטַן
תִּתְקַטֵּל	תַּקְטִיל	תָּקְטַל	תִּכְבַּד	תִּקְטַן
תִּתְקַטֵּל	תַּקְטִיל	תָּקְטַל	תִּכְבַּד	תִּקְטַן
תִּתְקַטְּלִי	תַּקְטִ֫ילִי	תָּקְטְלִי	תִּכְבְּדִי	תִּקְטְנִי
אֶתְקַטֵּל	אַקְטִיל	אָקְטַל	אֶכְבַּד	אֶקְטַן
יִתְקַטְּלוּ	יַקְטִ֫ילוּ	יָקְטְלוּ	יִכְבְּדוּ	יִקְטְנוּ
תִּתְקַטֵּ֫לְנָה	תַּקְטֵ֫לְנָה	תָּקְטַ֫לְנָה	תִּכְבַּ֫דְנָה	תִּקְטַ֫נָּה
תִּתְקַטְּלוּ	תַּקְטִ֫ילוּ	תָּקְטְלוּ	תִּכְבְּדוּ	תִּקְטְנוּ
תִּתְקַטֵּ֫לְנָה	תַּקְטֵ֫לְנָה	תָּקְטַ֫לְנָה	תִּכְבַּ֫דְנָה	תִּקְטַ֫נָּה
נִתְקַטֵּל	נַקְטִיל	נָקְטַל	נִכְבַּד	נִקְטַן
הִתְקַטֵּל	הַקְטֵל		כְּבַד	קְטַן
הִתְקַטְּלִי	הַקְטִ֫ילִי		כִּבְדִי	קִטְנִי
הִתְקַטְּלוּ	הַקְטִ֫ילוּ		כִּבְדוּ	קִטְנוּ
הִתְקַטֵּ֫לְנָה	הַקְטֵ֫לְנָה		כְּבַ֫דְנָה	קְטַ֫נָּה
הִתְקַטֹּל	הַקְטֵל	הָקְטֵל	כָּבוֹד	קָטוֹן
הִתְקַטֵּל	הַקְטִיל	הָקְטַל	כְּבֹד	קְטֹן
מִתְקַטֵּל	מַקְטִיל	מָקְטָל	כָּבֵד	קָטֹן
וַיִּתְקַטֵּל	וַיַּקְטֵל	וַיָּקְטַל	וַיִּכְבַּד	וַיִּקְטַן
יִתְקַטֵּל	יַקְטֵל	יָקְטַל	יִכְבַּד	יִקְטַן
אֶתְקַטְּלָה	אַקְטִ֫ילָה		אֶכְבְּדָה	אֶקְטְנָה

	Qal	Nip'al	Pi'ēl	Pu'al
Perfect				
3 m.s.	עָמַד	נֶעֱמַד	עִמֵּד	עֻמַּד
3 f.s.	עָמְדָה	נֶעֶמְדָה	עִמְּדָה	עֻמְּדָה
2 m.s.	עָמַדְתָּ	נֶעֱמַדְתָּ	עִמַּדְתָּ	עֻמַּדְתָּ
2 f.s.	עָמַדְתְּ	נֶעֱמַדְתְּ	עִמַּדְתְּ	עֻמַּדְתְּ
1 c.s.	עָמַדְתִּי	נֶעֱמַדְתִּי	עִמַּדְתִּי	עֻמַּדְתִּי
3 c.p.	עָמְדוּ	נֶעֶמְדוּ	עִמְּדוּ	עֻמְּדוּ
2 m.p.	עֲמַדְתֶּם	נֶעֱמַדְתֶּם	עִמַּדְתֶּם	עֻמַּדְתֶּם
2 f.p.	עֲמַדְתֶּן	נֶעֱמַדְתֶּן	עִמַּדְתֶּן	עֻמַּדְתֶּן
1 c.p.	עָמַדְנוּ	נֶעֱמַדְנוּ	עִמַּדְנוּ	עֻמַּדְנוּ
Imperfect				
3 m.s.	יַעֲמֹד	יֵעָמֵד	יְעַמֵּד	יְעֻמַּד
3 f.s.	תַּעֲמֹד	תֵּעָמֵד	תְּעַמֵּד	תְּעֻמַּד
2 m.s.	תַּעֲמֹד	תֵּעָמֵד	תְּעַמֵּד	תְּעֻמַּד
2 f.s.	תַּעַמְדִי	תֵּעָמְדִי	תְּעַמְּדִי	תְּעֻמְּדִי
1 c.s.	אֶעֱמֹד	אֵעָמֵד	אֲעַמֵּד	אֲעֻמַּד
3 m.p.	יַעַמְדוּ	יֵעָמְדוּ	יְעַמְּדוּ	יְעֻמְּדוּ
3 f.p.	תַּעֲמֹדְנָה	תֵּעָמַדְנָה	תְּעַמֵּדְנָה	תְּעֻמַּדְנָה
2 m.p.	תַּעַמְדוּ	תֵּעָמְדוּ	תְּעַמְּדוּ	תְּעֻמְּדוּ
2 f.p.	תַּעֲמֹדְנָה	תֵּעָמַדְנָה	תְּעַמֵּדְנָה	תְּעֻמַּדְנָה
1 c.p.	נַעֲמֹד	נֵעָמֵד	נְעַמֵּד	נְעֻמַּד
Imperative				
2 m.s.	עֲמֹד	הֵעָמֵד	עַמֵּד	
2 f.s.	עִמְדִי	הֵעָמְדִי	עַמְּדִי	
2 m.p.	עִמְדוּ	הֵעָמְדוּ	עַמְּדוּ	
2 f.p.	עֲמֹדְנָה	הֵעָמַדְנָה	עַמֵּדְנָה	
Infinitive				
Absolute	עָמוֹד	נַעֲמֹד	עַמֹּד	עֻמֹּד
Construct	עֲמֹד	הֵעָמֵד	עַמֵּד	עֻמַּד
Participle				
Active	עֹמֵד		מְעַמֵּד	
Passive	עָמוּד	נֶעֱמָד		מְעֻמָּד
Imperfect ו consecut.	וַיַּעֲמֹד	וַיֵּעָמֶד	וַיְעַמֵּד	וַיְעֻמַּד
Jussive	יַעֲמֹד	יֵעָמֶד	יְעַמֵּד	יְעֻמַּד
Cohortative	אֶעֶמְדָה	אֵעָמְדָה	אֲעַמְּדָה	

Refer to §48.

Hitpa‘ēl	Hip‘îl	Hop‘al	Stative Qal	
				Perfect
הִתְעַמֵּד	הֶעֱמִיד	הָעֳמַד	חָזַק	3 m.s.
הִתְעַמְּדָה	הֶעֱמִידָה	הָעָמְדָה	חָזְקָה	3 f.s.
הִתְעַמַּדְתָּ	הֶעֱמַדְתָּ	הָעֳמַדְתָּ	חָזַקְתָּ	2 m.s.
הִתְעַמַּדְתְּ	הֶעֱמַדְתְּ	הָעֳמַדְתְּ	חָזַקְתְּ	2 f.s.
הִתְעַמַּדְתִּי	הֶעֱמַדְתִּי	הָעֳמַדְתִּי	חָזַקְתִּי	1 c.s.
הִתְעַמְּדוּ	הֶעֱמִידוּ	הָעָמְדוּ	חָזְקוּ	3 c.p.
הִתְעַמַּדְתֶּם	הֶעֱמַדְתֶּם	הָעֳמַדְתֶּם	חֲזַקְתֶּם	2 m.p.
הִתְעַמַּדְתֶּן	הֶעֱמַדְתֶּן	הָעֳמַדְתֶּן	חֲזַקְתֶּן	2 f.p.
הִתְעַמַּדְנוּ	הֶעֱמַדְנוּ	הָעֳמַדְנוּ	חָזַקְנוּ	1 c.p.
				Imperfect
יִתְעַמֵּד	יַעֲמִיד	יָעֳמַד	יֶחֱזַק	3 m.s.
תִּתְעַמֵּד	תַּעֲמִיד	תָּעֳמַד	תֶּחֱזַק	3 f.s.
תִּתְעַמֵּד	תַּעֲמִיד	תָּעֳמַד	תֶּחֱזַק	2 m.s.
תִּתְעַמְּדִי	תַּעֲמִידִי	תָּעָמְדִי	תֶּחֶזְקִי	2 f.s.
אֶתְעַמֵּד	אַעֲמִיד	אָעֳמַד	אֶחֱזַק	1 c.s.
יִתְעַמְּדוּ	יַעֲמִידוּ	יָעָמְדוּ	יֶחֶזְקוּ	3 m.p.
תִּתְעַמֵּדְנָה	תַּעֲמֵדְנָה	תָּעֳמַדְנָה	תֶּחֱזַקְנָה	3 f.p.
תִּתְעַמְּדוּ	תַּעֲמִידוּ	תָּעָמְדוּ	תֶּחֶזְקוּ	2 m.p.
תִּתְעַמֵּדְנָה	תַּעֲמֵדְנָה	תָּעֳמַדְנָה	תֶּחֱזַקְנָה	2 f.p.
נִתְעַמֵּד	נַעֲמִיד	נָעֳמַד	נֶחֱזַק	1 c.p.
				Imperative
הִתְעַמֵּד	הַעֲמֵד		חֲזַק	2 m.s.
הִתְעַמְּדִי	הַעֲמִידִי		חִזְקִי	2 f.s.
הִתְעַמְּדוּ	הַעֲמִידוּ		חִזְקוּ	2 m.p.
הִתְעַמֵּדְנָה	הַעֲמֵדְנָה		חֲזַקְנָה	2 f.p.
				Infinitive
הִתְעַמֵּד	הַעֲמֵד	הָעֳמֵד	חָזוֹק	Absolute
הִתְעַמֵּד	הַעֲמִיד	הָעֳמַד	חֲזֹק	Construct
				Participle
מִתְעַמֵּד	מַעֲמִיד		חָזֵק	Active
		מָעֳמָד		Passive
וַיִּתְעַמֵּד	וַיַּעֲמֵד	וַיָּעֳמַד	וַיֶּחֱזַק	Imperfect ו consecut.
יִתְעַמֵּד	יַעֲמֵד	יָעֳמַד	יֶחֱזַק	Jussive
אֶתְעַמְּדָה	אַעֲמִידָה		אֶחֶזְקָה	Cohortative

	Qal	Nip'al	Pi'ēl	Pu'al
Perfect				
3 m.s.	גָּאַל	נִגְאַל	גֵּאֵל	גֹּאַל
3 f.s.	גָּאֲלָה	נִגְאֲלָה	גֵּאֲלָה	גֹּאֲלָה
2 m.s.	גָּאַלְתָּ	נִגְאַלְתָּ	גֵּאַלְתָּ	גֹּאַלְתָּ
2 f.s.	גָּאַלְתְּ	נִגְאַלְתְּ	גֵּאַלְתְּ	גֹּאַלְתְּ
1 c.s.	גָּאַלְתִּי	נִגְאַלְתִּי	גֵּאַלְתִּי	גֹּאַלְתִּי
3 c.p.	גָּאֲלוּ	נִגְאֲלוּ	גֵּאֲלוּ	גֹּאֲלוּ
2 m.p.	גְּאַלְתֶּם	נִגְאַלְתֶּם	גֵּאַלְתֶּם	גֹּאַלְתֶּם
2 f.p.	גְּאַלְתֶּן	נִגְאַלְתֶּן	גֵּאַלְתֶּן	גֹּאַלְתֶּן
1 c.p.	גָּאַלְנוּ	נִגְאַלְנוּ	גֵּאַלְנוּ	גֹּאַלְנוּ
Imperfect				
3 m.s.	יִגְאַל	יִגָּאֵל	יְגָאֵל	יְגֹאַל
3 f.s.	תִּגְאַל	תִּגָּאֵל	תְּגָאֵל	תְּגֹאַל
2 m.s.	תִּגְאַל	תִּגָּאֵל	תְּגָאֵל	תְּגֹאַל
2 f.s.	תִּגְאֲלִי	תִּגָּאֲלִי	תְּגָאֲלִי	תְּגֹאֲלִי
1 c.s.	אֶגְאַל	אֶגָּאֵל	אֲגָאֵל	אֲגֹאַל
3 m.p.	יִגְאֲלוּ	יִגָּאֲלוּ	יְגָאֲלוּ	יְגֹאֲלוּ
3 f.p.	תִּגְאַלְנָה	תִּגָּאַלְנָה	תְּגָאֵלְנָה	תְּגֹאַלְנָה
2 m.p.	תִּגְאֲלוּ	תִּגָּאֲלוּ	תְּגָאֲלוּ	תְּגֹאֲלוּ
2 f.p.	תִּגְאַלְנָה	תִּגָּאַלְנָה	תְּגָאֵלְנָה	תְּגֹאַלְנָה
1 c.p.	נִגְאַל	נִגָּאֵל	נְגָאֵל	נְגֹאַל
Imperative				
2 m.s.	גְּאַל	הִגָּאֵל	גָּאֵל	
2 f.s.	גַּאֲלִי	הִגָּאֲלִי	גָּאֲלִי	
2 m.p.	גַּאֲלוּ	הִגָּאֲלוּ	גָּאֲלוּ	
2 f.p.	גְּאַלְנָה	הִגָּאַלְנָה	גָּאֵלְנָה	
Infinitive				
Absolute	גָּאוֹל	נִגְאֹל	גָּאֵל	גֹּאַל
Construct	גְּאֹל	הִגָּאֵל	גָּאֵל	גֹּאַל
Participle				
Active	גֹּאֵל		מְגָאֵל	
Passive	גָּאוּל	נִגְאָל		מְגֹאָל
Imperfect ו consecut.	וַיִּגְאַל	וַיִּגָּאֶל	וַיְגָאֶל	וַיְגֹאַל
Jussive	יִגְאַל	יִגָּאֶל	יְגָאֶל	יְגֹאַל
Cohortative	אֶגְאֲלָה	אֶגָּאֲלָה	אֲגָאֲלָה	

Refer to §49.

Hitpa‘ēl	Hip‘îl	Hop‘al	
			Perfect
הִתְגָּאֵל	הִגְאִיל	הָגְאַל	3 m.s.
הִתְגָּאֲלָה	הִגְאִילָה	הָגְאֲלָה	3 f.s.
הִתְגָּאַלְתָּ	הִגְאַלְתָּ	הָגְאַלְתָּ	2 m.s.
הִתְגָּאַלְתְּ	הִגְאַלְתְּ	הָגְאַלְתְּ	2 f.s.
הִתְגָּאַלְתִּי	הִגְאַלְתִּי	הָגְאַלְתִּי	1 c.s.
הִתְגָּאֲלוּ	הִגְאִילוּ	הָגְאֲלוּ	3 c.p.
הִתְגָּאַלְתֶּם	הִגְאַלְתֶּם	הָגְאַלְתֶּם	2 m.p.
הִתְגָּאַלְתֶּן	הִגְאַלְתֶּן	הָגְאַלְתֶּן	2 f.p.
הִתְגָּאַלְנוּ	הִגְאַלְנוּ	הָגְאַלְנוּ	1 c.p.
			Imperfect
יִתְגָּאֵל.	יַגְאִיל	יָגְאַל	3 m.s.
תִּתְגָּאֵל	תַּגְאִיל	תָּגְאַל	3 f.s.
תִּתְגָּאֵל	תַּגְאִיל	תָּגְאַל	2 m.s.
תִּתְגָּאֲלִי	תַּגְאִילִי	תָּגְאֲלִי	2 f.s.
אֶתְגָּאֵל	אַגְאִיל	אָגְאַל	1 c.s.
יִתְגָּאֲלוּ	יַגְאִילוּ	יָגְאֲלוּ	3 m.p.
תִּתְגָּאֵלְנָה	תַּגְאֵלְנָה	תָּגְאַלְנָה	3 f.p.
תִּתְגָּאֲלוּ	תַּגְאִילוּ	תָּגְאֲלוּ	2 m.p.
תִּתְגָּאֵלְנָה	תַּגְאֵלְנָה	תָּגְאַלְנָה	2 f.p.
נִתְגָּאֵל	נַגְאִיל	נָגְאַל	1 c.p.
			Imperative
הִתְגָּאֵל	הַגְאֵל		2 m.s.
הִתְגָּאֲלִי	הַגְאִילִי		2 f.s.
הִתְגָּאֲלוּ	הַגְאִילוּ		2 m.p.
הִתְגָּאֵלְנָה	הַגְאֵלְנָה		2 f.p.
			Infinitive
חִתְגָּאֵל	חַגְאֵל	חָגְאֵל	Absolute
הִתְגָּאֵל	הַגְאִיל	הָגְאַל	Construct
			Participle
מִתְגָּאֵל	מַגְאִיל		Active
		מָגְאָל	Passive
וַיִּתְגָּאֶל	וַיַּגְאֵל	וַיָּגְאַל	Imperfect ו consecut.
יִתְגָּאֶל	יַגְאֵל	יָגְאַל	Jussive
אֶתְגָּאֲלָה	אַגְאִילָה		Cohortative

	Qal	Nip'al	Pi'ēl	Pu'al
Perfect				
3 m.s.	שָׁלַח	נִשְׁלַח	שִׁלַּח	שֻׁלַּח
3 f.s.	שָׁלְחָה	נִשְׁלְחָה	שִׁלְּחָה	שֻׁלְּחָה
2 m.s.	שָׁלַחְתָּ	נִשְׁלַחְתָּ	שִׁלַּחְתָּ	שֻׁלַּחְתָּ
2 f.s.	שָׁלַחַתְּ	נִשְׁלַחַתְּ	שִׁלַּחַתְּ	שֻׁלַּחַתְּ
1 c.s.	שָׁלַחְתִּי	נִשְׁלַחְתִּי	שִׁלַּחְתִּי	שֻׁלַּחְתִּי
3 c.p.	שָׁלְחוּ	נִשְׁלְחוּ	שִׁלְּחוּ	שֻׁלְּחוּ
2 m.p.	שְׁלַחְתֶּם	נִשְׁלַחְתֶּם	שִׁלַּחְתֶּם	שֻׁלַּחְתֶּם
2 f.p.	שְׁלַחְתֶּן	נִשְׁלַחְתֶּן	שִׁלַּחְתֶּן	שֻׁלַּחְתֶּן
1 c.p.	שָׁלַחְנוּ	נִשְׁלַחְנוּ	שִׁלַּחְנוּ	שֻׁלַּחְנוּ
Imperfect				
3 m.s.	יִשְׁלַח	יִשָּׁלַח	יְשַׁלַּח	יְשֻׁלַּח
3 f.s.	תִּשְׁלַח	תִּשָּׁלַח	תְּשַׁלַּח	תְּשֻׁלַּח
2 m.s.	תִּשְׁלַח	תִּשָּׁלַח	תְּשַׁלַּח	תְּשֻׁלַּח
2 f.s.	תִּשְׁלְחִי	תִּשָּׁלְחִי	תְּשַׁלְּחִי	תְּשֻׁלְּחִי
1 c.s.	אֶשְׁלַח	אֶשָּׁלַח	אֲשַׁלַּח	אֲשֻׁלַּח
3 m.p.	יִשְׁלְחוּ	יִשָּׁלְחוּ	יְשַׁלְּחוּ	יְשֻׁלְּחוּ
3 f.p.	תִּשְׁלַחְנָה	תִּשָּׁלַחְנָה	תְּשַׁלַּחְנָה	תְּשֻׁלַּחְנָה
2 m.p.	תִּשְׁלְחוּ	תִּשָּׁלְחוּ	תְּשַׁלְּחוּ	תְּשֻׁלְּחוּ
2 f.p.	תִּשְׁלַחְנָה	תִּשָּׁלַחְנָה	תְּשַׁלַּחְנָה	תְּשֻׁלַּחְנָה
1 c.p.	נִשְׁלַח	נִשָּׁלַח	נְשַׁלַּח	נְשֻׁלַּח
Imperative				
2 m.s.	שְׁלַח	הִשָּׁלַח	שַׁלַּח	
2 f.s.	שִׁלְחִי	הִשָּׁלְחִי	שַׁלְּחִי	
2 m.p.	שִׁלְחוּ	הִשָּׁלְחוּ	שַׁלְּחוּ	
2 f.p.	שְׁלַחְנָה	הִשָּׁלַחְנָה	שַׁלַּחְנָה	
Infinitive				
Absolute	שָׁלוֹחַ	נִשְׁלוֹחַ	שַׁלֵּחַ	שֻׁלֹּחַ
Construct	שְׁלֹחַ	הִשָּׁלַח	שַׁלַּח	שֻׁלַּח
Participle				
Active	שֹׁלֵחַ		מְשַׁלַּח	
Passive	שָׁלוּחַ	נִשְׁלָח		מְשֻׁלָּח
Imperfect ו consecut.	וַיִּשְׁלַח	וַיִּשָּׁלַח	וַיְשַׁלַּח	וַיְשֻׁלַּח
Jussive	יִשְׁלַח	יִשָּׁלַח	יְשַׁלַּח	יְשֻׁלַּח
Cohortative	אֶשְׁלְחָה	אֶשָּׁלְחָה	אֲשַׁלְּחָה	

Refer to §50.

Hitpa'ēl	Hip'îl	Hop'al	
			Perfect
הִשְׁתַּלַּח	הִשְׁלִיחַ	הָשְׁלַח	3 m.s.
הִשְׁתַּלְּחָה	הִשְׁלִיחָה	הָשְׁלְחָה	3 f.s.
הִשְׁתַּלַּחְתָּ	הִשְׁלַחְתָּ	הָשְׁלַחְתָּ	2 m.s.
הִשְׁתַּלַּחַתְּ	הִשְׁלַחַתְּ	הָשְׁלַחַתְּ	2 f.s.
הִשְׁתַּלַּחְתִּי	הִשְׁלַחְתִּי	הָשְׁלַחְתִּי	1 c.s.
הִשְׁתַּלְּחוּ	הִשְׁלִיחוּ	הָשְׁלְחוּ	3 c.p.
הִשְׁתַּלַּחְתֶּם	הִשְׁלַחְתֶּם	הָשְׁלַחְתֶּם	2 m.p.
הִשְׁתַּלַּחְתֶּן	הִשְׁלַחְתֶּן	הָשְׁלַחְתֶּן	2 f.p.
הִשְׁתַּלַּחְנוּ	הִשְׁלַחְנוּ	הָשְׁלַחְנוּ	1 c.p.
			Imperfect
יִשְׁתַּלַּח	יַשְׁלִיחַ	יָשְׁלַח	3 m.s.
תִּשְׁתַּלַּח	תַּשְׁלִיחַ	תָּשְׁלַח	3 f.s.
תִּשְׁתַּלַּח	תַּשְׁלִיחַ	תָּשְׁלַח	2 m.s.
תִּשְׁתַּלְּחִי	תַּשְׁלִיחִי	תָּשְׁלְחִי	2 f.s.
אֶשְׁתַּלַּח	אַשְׁלִיחַ	אָשְׁלַח	1 c.s.
יִשְׁתַּלְּחוּ	יַשְׁלִיחוּ	יָשְׁלְחוּ	3 m.p.
תִּשְׁתַּלַּחְנָה	תַּשְׁלַחְנָה	תָּשְׁלַחְנָה	3 f.p.
תִּשְׁתַּלְּחוּ	תַּשְׁלִיחוּ	תָּשְׁלְחוּ	2 m.p.
תִּשְׁתַּלַּחְנָה	תַּשְׁלַחְנָה	תָּשְׁלַחְנָה	2 f.p.
נִשְׁתַּלַּח	נַשְׁלִיחַ	נָשְׁלַח	1 c.p.
			Imperative
הִשְׁתַּלַּח	הַשְׁלַח		2 m.s.
הִשְׁתַּלְּחִי	הַשְׁלִיחִי		2 f.s.
הִשְׁתַּלְּחוּ	הַשְׁלִיחוּ		2 m.p.
הִשְׁתַּלַּחְנָה	הַשְׁלַחְנָה		2 f.p.
			Infinitive
הִשְׁתַּלֹּחַ	הַשְׁלֵחַ	הָשְׁלֵחַ	Absolute
הִשְׁתַּלַּח	הַשְׁלִיחַ	הָשְׁלַח	Construct
			Participle
מִשְׁתַּלֵּחַ	מַשְׁלִיחַ		Active
		מָשְׁלָח	Passive
וַיִּשְׁתַּלַּח	וַיַּשְׁלַח	וַיָּשְׁלַח	Imperfect ו consecut.
יִשְׁתַּלַּח	יַשְׁלַח	יָשְׁלַח	Jussive
אֶשְׁתַּלְּחָה	אַשְׁלִיחָה		Cohortative

	Qal	Nipʿal	Piʿēl
Perfect			
3 m.s.	אָכַל		
3 f.s.	אָֽכְלָה		
2 m.s.	אָכַלְתָּ		
2 f.s.	אָכַלְתְּ		
1 c.s.	אָכַלְתִּי		
3 c.p.	אָֽכְלוּ		
2 m.p.	אֲכַלְתֶּם		
2 f.p.	אֲכַלְתֶּן		
1 c.p.	אָכַלְנוּ		
Imperfect			
3 m.s.	יֹאכַל		
3 f.s.	תֹּאכַל		
2 m.s.	תֹּאכַל		
2 f.s.	תֹּֽאכְלִי		
1 c.s.	אֹכַל		
3 m.p.	יֹֽאכְלוּ		
3 f.p.	תֹּאכַלְנָה		
2 m.p.	תֹּֽאכְלוּ		
2 f.p.	תֹּאכַלְנָה		
1 c.p.	נֹאכַל		
Imperative			
2 m.s.	אֱכֹל		
2 f.s.	אִכְלִי		
2 m.p.	אִכְלוּ		
2 f.p.	אֱכֹלְנָה		
Infinitive			
Absolute	אָכוֹל		
Construct	אֱכֹל		
Participle			
Active	אֹכֵל		
Passive	אָכוּל		
Imperfect ו consecut.	וַיֹּאכַל (וָאֹכֵל)		
Jussive	יֹאכַל		
Cohortative	אֹכְלָה		

Refer to §51. Since the remaining conjugations of the פ"א verb are the same as the פ laryngeal

Puʻal	Hitpaʻēl	Hipʻîl	Hopʻal	
				Perfect 3 m.s. 3 f.s. 2 m.s. 2 f.s. 1 c.s. 3 c.p. 2 m.p. 2 f.p. 1 c.p.
				Imperfect 3 m.s. 3 f.s. 2 m.s. 2 f.s. 1 c.s. 3 m.p. 3 f.p. 2 m.p. 2 f.p. 1 c.p.
				Imperative 2 m.s. 2 f.s. 2 m.p. 2 f.p.
				Infinitive Absolute Construct
				Participle Active Passive
				Imperfect ו consecut.
				Jussive
				Cohortative

verb, they are not listed on these pages.

	Qal	Nip'al	Pi'ēl	Pu'al.
Perfect				
3 m.s.	גָּלָה	נִגְלָה	גִּלָּה	גֻּלָּה
3 f.s.	גָּלְתָה	נִגְלְתָה	גִּלְּתָה	גֻּלְּתָה
2 m.s.	גָּלִיתָ	נִגְלֵיתָ	גִּלִּיתָ	גֻּלֵּיתָ
2 f.s.	גָּלִית	נִגְלֵית	גִּלִּית	גֻּלֵּית
1 c.s.	גָּלִיתִי	נִגְלֵיתִי	גִּלִּיתִי	גֻּלֵּיתִי
3 c.p.	גָּלוּ	נִגְלוּ	גִּלּוּ	גֻּלּוּ
2 m.p.	גְּלִיתֶם	נִגְלֵיתֶם	גִּלִּיתֶם	גֻּלֵּיתֶם
2 f.p.	גְּלִיתֶן	נִגְלֵיתֶן	גִּלִּיתֶן	גֻּלֵּיתֶן
1 c.p.	גָּלִינוּ	נִגְלֵינוּ	גִּלִּינוּ	גֻּלֵּינוּ
Imperfect				
3 m.s.	יִגְלֶה	יִגָּלֶה	יְגַלֶּה	יְגֻלֶּה
3 f.s.	תִּגְלֶה	תִּגָּלֶה	תְּגַלֶּה	תְּגֻלֶּה
2 m.s.	תִּגְלֶה	תִּגָּלֶה	תְּגַלֶּה	תְּגֻלֶּה
2 f.s.	תִּגְלִי	תִּגָּלִי	תְּגַלִּי	תְּגֻלִּי
1 c.s.	אֶגְלֶה	אֶגָּלֶה	אֲגַלֶּה	אֲגֻלֶּה
3 m.p.	יִגְלוּ	יִגָּלוּ	יְגַלּוּ	יְגֻלּוּ
3 f.p.	תִּגְלֶינָה	תִּגָּלֶינָה	תְּגַלֶּינָה	תְּגֻלֶּינָה
2 m.p.	תִּגְלוּ	תִּגָּלוּ	תְּגַלּוּ	תְּגֻלּוּ
2 f.p.	תִּגְלֶינָה	תִּגָּלֶינָה	תְּגַלֶּינָה	תְּגֻלֶּינָה
1 c.p.	נִגְלֶה	נִגָּלֶה	נְגַלֶּה	נְגֻלֶּה
Imperative				
2 m.s.	גְּלֵה	הִגָּלֵה	גַּלֵּה	
2 f.s.	גְּלִי	הִגָּלִי	גַּלִּי	
2 m.p.	גְּלוּ	הִגָּלוּ	גַּלּוּ	
2 f.p.	גְּלֶינָה	הִגָּלֶינָה	גַּלֶּינָה	
Infinitive				
Absolute	גָּלֹה	נִגְלֹה	גַּלֹּה	גֻּלֹּה
Construct	גְּלוֹת	הִגָּלוֹת	גַּלּוֹת	גֻּלּוֹת
Participle				
Active	גֹּלֶה		מְגַלֶּה	
Passive	גָּלוּי	נִגְלֶה		מְגֻלֶּה
Imperfect ו consecut.	וַיִּגֶל	וַיִּגָּל	וַיְגַל	וַיְגֻל
Jussive	יִגֶל	יִגָּל	יְגַל	יְגֻל
Cohortative	See §52.6			

Refer to §52.

Hitpa'ēl	Hip'îl	Hop'al	היה Qal
הִתְגַּלָּה	הִגְלָה	הָגְלָה	הָיָה
הִתְגַּלְּתָה	הִגְלְתָה	הָגְלְתָה	הָֽיְתָה
הִתְגַּלִּיתָ	הִגְלִיתָ	הָגְלֵיתָ	הָיִיתָ
הִתְגַּלִּית	הִגְלִית	הָגְלֵית	הָיִית
הִתְגַּלִּיתִי	הִגְלִיתִי	הָגְלֵיתִי	הָיִיתִי
הִתְגַּלּוּ	הִגְלוּ	הָגְלוּ	הָיוּ
הִתְגַּלִּיתֶם	הִגְלִיתֶם	הָגְלֵיתֶם	הֱיִיתֶם
הִתְגַּלִּיתֶן	הִגְלִיתֶן	הָגְלֵיתֶן	הֱיִיתֶן
הִתְגַּלִּינוּ	הִגְלִינוּ	הָגְלֵינוּ	הָיִינוּ
יִתְגַּלֶּה	יַגְלֶה	יָגְלֶה	יִהְיֶה
תִּתְגַּלֶּה	תַּגְלֶה	תָּגְלֶה	תִּהְיֶה
תִּתְגַּלֶּה	תַּגְלֶה	תָּגְלֶה	תִּהְיֶה
תִּתְגַּלִּי	תַּגְלִי	תָּגְלִי	תִּהְיִי
אֶתְגַּלֶּה	אַגְלֶה	אָגְלֶה	אֶהְיֶה
יִתְגַּלּוּ	יַגְלוּ	יָגְלוּ	יִהְיוּ
תִּתְגַּלֶּינָה	תַּגְלֶינָה	תָּגְלֶינָה	תִּהְיֶינָה
תִּתְגַּלּוּ	תַּגְלוּ	תָּגְלוּ	תִּהְיוּ
תִּתְגַּלֶּינָה	תַּגְלֶינָה	תָּגְלֶינָה	תִּהְיֶינָה
נִתְגַּלֶּה	נַגְלֶה	נָגְלֶה	נִהְיֶה
הִתְגַּלֵּה	הַגְלֵה		הֱיֵה
הִתְגַּלִּי	הַגְלִי		הֲיִי
הִתְגַּלּוּ	הַגְלוּ		הֲיוּ
הִתְגַּלֶּינָה	הַגְלֶינָה		הֱיֶינָה
הִתְגַּלֹּה	הַגְלֵה	הָגְלֵה	הָיֹה, הָיוֹ
הִתְגַּלּוֹת	הַגְלוֹת	הָגְלוֹת	הֱיוֹת
מִתְגַּלֶּה	מַגְלֶה		הוֹיֶה
		מָגְלֶה	
וַיִּתְגַּל	וַיֶּגֶל		וַיְהִי
יִתְגַּל	יֶגֶל		יְהִי

<u>Table of Suffixes to</u>

	Qal Perfect גָּלָה	Qal Imperfect יִגְלֶה
Suffixes		
1 c.s.	גָּלַנִי	יִגְלֵנִי
2 m.s.	גָּלְךָ	יִגְלְךָ
2 f.s.	גָּלָךְ	יִגְלֵךְ
3 m.s.	גָּלָהוּ	יִגְלֵהוּ
3 f.s.	גָּלָהּ	יִגְלֶהָ
1 c.p.	גָּלָנוּ	יִגְלֵנוּ
2 m.p.	גֳּלְכֶם	יִגְלְכֶם
2 f.p.	גֳּלְכֶן	יִגְלְכֶן
3 m.p.	גָּלָם	יִגְלֵם
3 f.p.	גָּלָן	יִגְלֵן

ל"ה Verb Forms and Infinitive

Qal Imperative גְּלֵה	Qal Inf. Const. גְּלוֹת	Suffixes
גְּלֵ֫נִי	גְּלוֹתִי	1 c.s.
גְּלֶ֫ךָ	גְּלֽוֹתְךָ	2 m.s.
גְּלֵךְ	גְּלוֹתֵךְ	2 f.s.
גְּלֵ֫הוּ	גְּלוֹתוֹ	3 m.s.
גְּלֶ֫הָ	גְּלוֹתָהּ	3 f.s.
גְּלֵ֫נוּ	גְּלוֹתֵ֫נוּ	1 c.p.
גְּלֵכֶם	גְּלֽוֹתְכֶם	2 m.p.
גְּלֵכֶן	גְּלֽוֹתְכֶן	2 f.p.
גְּלֵם	גְּלוֹתָם	3 m.p.
גְּלֵן	גְּלוֹתָן	3 f.p.

	Qal	Nip'al	Pi'ēl	Pu'āl
Perfect				
3 m.s.	מָצָא	נִמְצָא	מִצֵּא	מֻצָּא
3 f.s.	מָצְאָה	נִמְצְאָה	מִצְּאָה	מֻצְּאָה
2 m.s.	מָצָאתָ	נִמְצֵאתָ	מִצֵּאתָ	מֻצֵּאתָ
2 f.s.	מָצָאת	נִמְצֵאת	מִצֵּאת	מֻצֵּאת
1 c.s.	מָצָאתִי	נִמְצֵאתִי	מִצֵּאתִי	מֻצֵּאתִי
3 c.p.	מָצְאוּ	נִמְצְאוּ	מִצְּאוּ	מֻצְּאוּ
2 m.p.	מְצָאתֶם	נִמְצֵאתֶם	מִצֵּאתֶם	מֻצֵּאתֶם
2 f.p.	מְצָאתֶן	נִמְצֵאתֶן	מִצֵּאתֶן	מֻצֵּאתֶן
1 c.p.	מָצָאנוּ	נִמְצֵאנוּ	מִצֵּאנוּ	מֻצֵּאנוּ
Imperfect				
3 m.s.	יִמְצָא	יִמָּצֵא	יְמַצֵּא	יְמֻצָּא
3 f.s.	תִּמְצָא	תִּמָּצֵא	תְּמַצֵּא	תְּמֻצָּא
2 m.s.	תִּמְצָא	תִּמָּצֵא	תְּמַצֵּא	תְּמֻצָּא
2 f.s.	תִּמְצְאִי	תִּמָּצְאִי	תְּמַצְּאִי	תְּמֻצְּאִי
1 c.s.	אֶמְצָא	אֶמָּצֵא	אֲמַצֵּא	אֲמֻצָּא
3 m.p.	יִמְצְאוּ	יִמָּצְאוּ	יְמַצְּאוּ	יְמֻצְּאוּ
3 f.p.	תִּמְצֶאנָה	תִּמָּצֶאנָה	תְּמַצֶּאנָה	תְּמֻצֶּאנָה
2 m.p.	תִּמְצְאוּ	תִּמָּצְאוּ	תְּמַצְּאוּ	תְּמֻצְּאוּ
2 f.p.	תִּמְצֶאנָה	תִּמָּצֶאנָה	תְּמַצֶּאנָה	תְּמֻצֶּאנָה
1 c.p.	נִמְצָא	נִמָּצֵא	נְמַצֵּא	נְמֻצָּא
Imperative				
2 m.s.	מְצָא	הִמָּצֵא	מַצֵּא	
2 f.s.	מִצְאִי	הִמָּצְאִי	מַצְּאִי	
2 m.p.	מִצְאוּ	הִמָּצְאוּ	מַצְּאוּ	
2 f.p.	מְצֶאנָה	הִמָּצֶאנָה	מַצֶּאנָה	
Infinitive				
Absolute	מָצוֹא	נִמְצֹא	מַצֹּא	מֻצֹּא
Construct	מְצֹא	הִמָּצֵא	מַצֵּא	מֻצָּא
Participle				
Active	מֹצֵא		מְמַצֵּא	
Passive	מָצוּא	נִמְצָא		מְמֻצָּא
Imperfect ו consecut.	וַיִּמְצָא	וַיִּמָּצֵא	וַיְמַצֵּא	וַיְמֻצָּא
Jussive	יִמְצָא	יִמָּצֵא	יְמַצֵּא	יְמֻצָּא
Cohortative	אֶמְצְאָה	אֶמָּצְאָה	אֲמַצְּאָה	

Refer to §53.

Hitpa'ēl	Hip'îl	Hop'al	Stative Qal	
				Perfect
הִתְמַצֵּא	הִמְצִיא	הֻמְצָא	מָלֵא	3 m.s.
הִתְמַצְּאָה	הִמְצִיאָה	הֻמְצְאָה	מָֽלְאָה	3 f.s.
הִתְמַצֵּאתָ	הִמְצֵאתָ	הֻמְצֵאתָ	מָלֵאתָ	2 m.s.
הִתְמַצֵּאת	הִמְצֵאת	הֻמְצֵאת	מָלֵאת	2 f.s.
הִתְמַצֵּאתִי	הִמְצֵאתִי	הֻמְצֵאתִי	מָלֵאתִי	1 c.s.
הִתְמַצְּאוּ	הִמְצִיאוּ	הֻמְצְאוּ	מָֽלְאוּ	3 c.p.
הִתְמַצֵּאתֶם	הִמְצֵאתֶם	הֻמְצֵאתֶם	מְלֵאתֶם	2 m.p.
הִתְמַצֵּאתֶן	הִמְצֵאתֶן	הֻמְצֵאתֶן	מְלֵאתֶן	2 f.p.
הִתְמַצֵּאנוּ	הִמְצֵאנוּ	הֻמְצֵאנוּ	מָלֵאנוּ	1 c.p.
				Imperfect
יִתְמַצֵּא	יַמְצִיא	יֻמְצָא	יִמְלָא	3 m.s.
תִּתְמַצֵּא	תַּמְצִיא	תֻּמְצָא	תִּמְלָא	3 f.s.
תִּתְמַצֵּא	תַּמְצִיא	תֻּמְצָא	תִּמְלָא	2 m.s.
תִּתְמַצְּאִי	תַּמְצִיאִי	תֻּמְצְאִי	תִּמְלְאִי	2 f.s.
אֶתְמַצֵּא	אַמְצִיא	אֻמְצָא	אֶמְלָא	1 c.s.
יִתְמַצְּאוּ	יַמְצִיאוּ	יֻמְצְאוּ	יִמְלְאוּ	3 m.p.
תִּתְמַצֶּאנָה	תַּמְצֶאנָה	תֻּמְצֶאנָה	תִּמְלֶאנָה	3 f.p.
תִּתְמַצְּאוּ	תַּמְצִיאוּ	תֻּמְצְאוּ	תִּמְלְאוּ	2 m.p.
תִּתְמַצֶּאנָה	תַּמְצֶאנָה	תֻמְצֶאנָה	תִּמְלֶאנָה	2 f.p.
נִתְמַצֵּא	נַמְצִיא	נֻמְצָא	נִמְלָא	1 c.p.
				Imperative
הִתְמַצֵּא	הַמְצֵא		מְלָא	2 m.s.
הִתְמַצְּאִי	הַמְצִיאִי		מִלְאִי	2 f.s.
הִתְמַצְּאוּ	הַמְצִיאוּ		מִלְאוּ	2 m.p.
הִתְמַצֶּאנָה	הַמְצֶאנָה		מְלֶאנָה	2 f.p.
				Infinitive
הִתְמַצֵּא	הַמְצֵא	הֻמְצֵא	מָלוֹא	Absolute
הִתְמַצֵּא	הַמְצִיא	הֻמְצָא	מְלֹא	Construct
				Participle
מִתְמַצֵּא	מַמְצִיא		מָלֵא	Active
		מֻמְצָא		Passive
וַיִּתְמַצֵּא	וַיַּמְצֵא	וַיֻּמְצָא	וַיִּמְלָא	Imperfect ו consecut.
יִתְמַצֵּא	יַמְצֵא	יֻמְצָא	יִמְלָא	Jussive
אֶתְמַצְּאָה	אַמְצִיאָה		אֶמְלְאָה	Cohortative

פ"י Verb
(Original פ"ו)

	Qal	Nip‘al	Pi‘ēl	Pu‘al
Perfect				
3 m.s.	יָלַד	נוֹלַד	יִלֵּד	יֻלַּד
3 f.s.	יָלְדָה	נוֹלְדָה	יִלְּדָה	יֻלְּדָה
2 m.s.	יָלַדְתָּ	נוֹלַדְתָּ	יִלַּדְתָּ	יֻלַּדְתָּ
2 f.s.	יָלַדְתְּ	נוֹלַדְתְּ	יִלַּדְתְּ	יֻלַּדְתְּ
1 c.s.	יָלַדְתִּי	נוֹלַדְתִּי	יִלַּדְתִּי	יֻלַּדְתִּי
3 c.p.	יָלְדוּ	נוֹלְדוּ	יִלְּדוּ	יֻלְּדוּ
2 m.p.	יְלַדְתֶּם	נוֹלַדְתֶּם	יִלַּדְתֶּם	יֻלַּדְתֶּם
2 f.p.	יְלַדְתֶּן	נוֹלַדְתֶּן	יִלַּדְתֶּן	יֻלַּדְתֶּן
1 c.p.	יָלַדְנוּ	נוֹלַדְנוּ	יִלַּדְנוּ	יֻלַּדְנוּ
Imperfect				
3 m.s.	יֵלֵד	יִוָּלֵד	יְוַלֵּד	יְוֻלַּד
3 f.s.	תֵּלֵד	תִּוָּלֵד	תְּוַלֵּד	תְּוֻלַּד
2 m.s.	תֵּלֵד	תִּוָּלֵד	תְּוַלֵּד	תְּוֻלַּד
2 f.s.	תֵּלְדִי	תִּוָּלְדִי	תְּוַלְּדִי	תְּוֻלְּדִי
1 c.s.	אֵלֵד	אֶוָּלֵד	אֲוַלֵּד	אֲוֻלַּד
3 m.p.	יֵלְדוּ	יִוָּלְדוּ	יְוַלְּדוּ	יְוֻלְּדוּ
3 f.p.	תֵּלַדְנָה	תִּוָּלַדְנָה	תְּוַלֵּדְנָה	תְּוֻלַּדְנָה
2 m.p.	תֵּלְדוּ	תִּוָּלְדוּ	תְּוַלְּדוּ	תְּוֻלְּדוּ
2 f.p.	תֵּלַדְנָה	תִּוָּלַדְנָה	תְּוַלֵּדְנָה	תְּוֻלַּדְנָה
1 c.p.	נֵלֵד	נִוָּלֵד	נְוַלֵּד	נְוֻלַּד
Imperative				
2 m.s.	לֵד	הִוָּלֵד	יַלֵּד	
2 f.s.	לְדִי	הִוָּלְדִי	יַלְּדִי	
2 m.p.	לְדוּ	הִוָּלְדוּ	יַלְּדוּ	
2 f.p.	לֵדְנָה	הִוָּלַדְנָה	יַלֵּדְנָה	
Infinitive				
Absolute	יָלוֹד	הִוָּלֹד	יַלֵּד	יֻלֹּד
Construct	לֶדֶת	הִוָּלֵד	יַלֵּד	יֻלַּד
Participle				
Active	יֹלֵד		מְוַלֵּד	
Passive	יָלוּד	נוֹלָד		מְוֻלָּד
Imperfect ו consecut.	וַיֵּלֶד	וַיִּוָּלֶד	וַיְוַלֵּד	וַיְוֻלַּד
Jussive	יֵלֶד	יִוָּלֶד	יְוַלֵּד	יְוֻלַּד
Cohortative	אֵלְדָה	אֶוָּלְדָה	אֲוַלְּדָה	

Refer to §54.

Hitpa'ēl	Hip'îl	Hop'al	Stative Qal	הלך Qal
הִתְוַלֵּד	הוֹלִיד	הוּלַד	יָרֵא	הָלַךְ
הִתְוַלְּדָה	הוֹלִידָה	הֽוּלְדָה	יָֽרְאָה	הָֽלְכָה
הִתְוַלַּדְתָּ	הוֹלַדְתָּ	הוּלַדְתָּ	יָרֵאתָ	הָלַכְתָּ
הִתְוַלַּדְתְּ	הוֹלַדְתְּ	הוּלַדְתְּ	יָרֵאת	הָלַכְתְּ
הִתְוַלַּדְתִּי	הוֹלַדְתִּי	הוּלַדְתִּי	יָרֵאתִי	הָלַכְתִּי
הִתְוַלְּדוּ	הוֹלִידוּ	הֽוּלְדוּ	יָֽרְאוּ	הָֽלְכוּ
הִתְוַלַּדְתֶּם	הֽוֹלַדְתֶּם	הֽוּלַדְתֶּם	יְרֵאתֶם	הֲלַכְתֶּם
הִתְוַלַּדְתֶּן	הֽוֹלַדְתֶּן	הֽוּלַדְתֶּן	יְרֵאתֶן	הֲלַכְתֶּן
הִתְוַלַּדְנוּ	הוֹלַדְנוּ	הוּלַדְנוּ	יָרֵאנוּ	הָלַכְנוּ
יִתְיַלֵּד	יוֹלִיד	יוּלַד	יִירָא	יֵלֵךְ
תִּתְיַלֵּד	תּוֹלִיד	תּוּלַד	תִּירָא	תֵּלֵךְ
תִּתְיַלֵּד	תּוֹלִיד	תּוּלַד	תִּירָא	תֵּלֵךְ
תִּתְיַלְּדִי	תּוֹלִידִי	תּֽוּלְדִי	תִּֽירְאִי	תֵּֽלְכִי
אֶתְיַלֵּד	אוֹלִיד	אוּלַד	אִירָא	אֵלֵךְ
יִתְיַלְּדוּ	יוֹלִידוּ	יֽוּלְדוּ	יִֽירְאוּ	יֵֽלְכוּ
תִּתְיַלֵּדְנָה	תּוֹלֵדְנָה	תּוּלַדְנָה	תִּירֶאנָה	תֵּלַכְנָה
תִּתְיַלְּדוּ	תּוֹלִידוּ	תּֽוּלְדוּ	תִּֽירְאוּ	תֵּֽלְכוּ
תִּתְיַלֵּדְנָה	תּוֹלֵדְנָה	תּוּלַדְנָה	תִּירֶאנָה	תֵּלַכְנָה
נִתְיַלֵּד	נוֹלִיד	נוּלַד	נִירָא	נֵלֵךְ
הִתְוַלֵּד	הוֹלֵד		יְרָא	לֵךְ
הִתְוַלְּדִי	הוֹלִידִי		יִרְאִי	לְכִי
הִתְוַלְּדוּ	הוֹלִידוּ		יִרְאוּ	לְכוּ
הִתְוַלֵּדְנָה	הוֹלֵדְנָה		יְרֶאנָה	לֵכְנָה
הִתְוַלֹּד	הוֹלֵד	הוּלֵד	יָרוֹא	הָלוֹךְ
הִתְוַלֵּד	הוֹלִיד	הוּלַד	יְרֹא	לֶכֶת
מִתְיַלֵּד	מוֹלִיד		יָרֵא	הֹלֵךְ
		מוּלָד		הָלוּךְ
וַיִּתְיַלֵּד	וַיּוֹלֶד	וַיּוּלַד	וַיִּירָא	וַיֵּלֶךְ
יִתְיַלֵּד	יוֹלֶד	יוּלַד	יִירָא	יֵלֶךְ
אֶתְיַלְּדָה	אוֹלִידָה		אִֽירְאָה	אֵֽלְכָה

Note: The intensive forms rarely occur.

פ"י Verb
(Original פ"י)

	Qal	Nip'al	Pi'ēl	Pu'al
Perfect				
3 m.s.	יָטַב	נוֹטַב	יִטֵּב	יֻטַּב
3 f.s.	יָטְבָה	נוֹטְבָה	יִטְּבָה	יֻטְּבָה
2 m.s.	יָטַבְתָּ	נוֹטַבְתָּ	יִטַּבְתָּ	יֻטַּבְתָּ
2 f.s.	יָטַבְתְּ	נוֹטַבְתְּ	יִטַּבְתְּ	יֻטַּבְתְּ
1 c.s.	יָטַבְתִּי	נוֹטַבְתִּי	יִטַּבְתִּי	יֻטַּבְתִּי
3 c.p.	יָטְבוּ	נוֹטְבוּ	יִטְּבוּ	יֻטְּבוּ
2 m.p.	יְטַבְתֶּם	נוֹטַבְתֶּם	יִטַּבְתֶּם	יֻטַּבְתֶּם
2 f.p.	יְטַבְתֶּן	נוֹטַבְתֶּן	יִטַּבְתֶּן	יֻטַּבְתֶּן
1 c.p.	יָטַבְנוּ	נוֹטַבְנוּ	יִטַּבְנוּ	יֻטַּבְנוּ
Imperfect				
3 m.s.	יִיטַב	יִוָּטֵב	יְיַטֵּב	יְיֻטַּב
3 f.s.	תִּיטַב	תִּוָּטֵב	תְּיַטֵּב	תְּיֻטַּב
2 m.s.	תִּיטַב	תִּוָּטֵב	תְּיַטֵּב	תְּיֻטַּב
2 f.s.	תִּיטְבִי	תִּוָּטְבִי	תְּיַטְּבִי	תְּיֻטְּבִי
1 c.s.	אִיטַב	אֶוָּטֵב	אֲיַטֵּב	אֲיֻטַּב
3 m.p.	יִיטְבוּ	יִוָּטְבוּ	יְיַטְּבוּ	יְיֻטְּבוּ
3 f.p.	תִּיטַבְנָה	תִּוָּטַבְנָה	תְּיַטֵּבְנָה	תְּיֻטַּבְנָה
2 m.p.	תִּיטְבוּ	תִּוָּטְבוּ	תְּיַטְּבוּ	תְּיֻטְּבוּ
2 f.p.	תִּיטַבְנָה	תִּוָּטַבְנָה	תְּיַטֵּבְנָה	תְּיֻטַּבְנָה
1 c.p.	נִיטַב	נִוָּטֵב	נְיַטֵּב	נְיֻטַּב
Imperative				
2 m.s.	יְטַב	הִוָּטֵב	יַטֵּב	
2 f.s.	יִטְבִי	הִוָּטְבִי	יַטְּבִי	
2 m.p.	יִטְבוּ	הִוָּטְבוּ	יַטְּבוּ	
2 f.p.	יְטַבְנָה	הִוָּטַבְנָה	יַטֵּבְנָה	
Infinitive				
Absolute	יָטוֹב	הִוָּטֹב	יַטֹּב	יֻטֹּב
Construct	יְטֹב	הִוָּטֵב	יַטֵּב	יֻטַּב
Participle				
Active	יֹטֵב		מְיַטֵּב	
Passive	יָטוּב	נוֹטָב		מְיֻטָּב
Imperfect ו consecut.	וַיִּיטַב	וַיִּוָּטֶב	וַיְיַטֵּב	וַיְיֻטַּב
Jussive	יִיטַב	יִוָּטֶב	יְיַטֵּב	יְיֻטַּב
Cohortative	אִיטְבָה	אֶוָּטְבָה	אֲיַטְּבָה	

Refer to §54.

Hitpa‘el	Hip‘îl	Hop‘al	
הִתְיַטֵּב	הֵיטִיב	הוּטַב	Perfect 3 m.s.
הִתְיַטְּבָה	הֵיטִיבָה	הוּטְבָה	3 f.s.
הִתְיַטַּבְתָּ	הֵיטַבְתָּ	הוּטַבְתָּ	2 m.s.
הִתְיַטַּבְתְּ	הֵיטַבְתְּ	הוּטַבְתְּ	2 f.s.
הִתְיַטַּבְתִּי	הֵיטַבְתִּי	הוּטַבְתִּי	1 c.s.
הִתְיַטְּבוּ	הֵיטִיבוּ	הוּטְבוּ	3 c.p.
הִתְיַטַּבְתֶּם	הֵיטַבְתֶּם	הוּטַבְתֶּם	2 m.p.
הִתְיַטַּבְתֶּן	הֵיטַבְתֶּן	הוּטַבְתֶּן	2 f.p.
הִתְיַטַּבְנוּ	הֵיטַבְנוּ	הוּטַבְנוּ	1 c.p.
			Imperfect
יִתְיַטֵּב	יֵיטִיב	יוּטַב	3 m.s.
תִּתְיַטֵּב	תֵּיטִיב	תּוּטַב	3 f.s.
תִּתְיַטֵּב	תֵּיטִיב	תּוּטַב	2 m.s.
תִּתְיַטְּבִי	תֵּיטִיבִי	תּוּטְבִי	2 f.s.
אֶתְיַטֵּב	אֵיטִיב	אוּטַב	1 c.s.
יִתְיַטְּבוּ	יֵיטִיבוּ	יוּטְבוּ	3 m.p.
תִּתְיַטֵּבְנָה	תֵּיטֵבְנָה	תּוּטַבְנָה	3 f.p.
תִּתְיַטְּבוּ	תֵּיטִיבוּ	תּוּטְבוּ	2 m.p.
תִּתְיַטֵּבְנָה	תֵּיטֵבְנָה	תּוּטַבְנָה	2 f.p.
נִתְיַטֵּב	נֵיטִיב	נוּטַב	1 c.p.
			Imperative
הִתְיַטֵּב	הֵיטֵב		2 m.s.
הִתְיַטְּבִי	הֵיטִיבִי		2 f.s.
הִתְיַטְּבוּ	הֵיטִיבוּ		2 m.p.
הִתְיַטֵּבְנָה	הֵיטֵבְנָה		2 f.p.
			Infinitive
הִתְיַטֹּב	הֵיטֵב	הוּטֵב	Absolute
הִתְיַטֵּב	הֵיטִיב	הוּטַב	Construct
			Participle
מִתְיַטֵּב	מֵיטִיב		Active
		מוּטָב	Passive
וַיִּתְיַטֵּב	וַיֵּיטֶב	וַיּוּטַב	Imperfect ו consecut.
יִתְיַטֵּב	יֵיטֶב	יוּטַב	Jussive
אֶתְיַטְּבָה	אֵיטִיבָה		Cohortative

	Qal		Nip'al	Pi'ēl	Pu'al
Perfect					
3 m.s.	נָגַשׁ	נָפַל	נִגַּשׁ	נִגַּשׁ	נֻגַּשׁ
3 f.s.	נָגְשָׁה	נָפְלָה	נִגְּשָׁה	נִגְּשָׁה	נֻגְּשָׁה
2 m.s.	נָגַשְׁתָּ	נָפַלְתָּ	נִגַּשְׁתָּ	נִגַּשְׁתָּ	נֻגַּשְׁתָּ
2 f.s.	נָגַשְׁתְּ	נָפַלְתְּ	נִגַּשְׁתְּ	נִגַּשְׁתְּ	נֻגַּשְׁתְּ
1 c.s.	נָגַשְׁתִּי	נָפַלְתִּי	נִגַּשְׁתִּי	נִגַּשְׁתִּי	נֻגַּשְׁתִּי
3 c.p.	נָגְשׁוּ	נָפְלוּ	נִגְּשׁוּ	נִגְּשׁוּ	נֻגְּשׁוּ
2 m.p.	נְגַשְׁתֶּם	נְפַלְתֶּם	נִגַּשְׁתֶּם	נִגַּשְׁתֶּם	נֻגַּשְׁתֶּם
2 f.p.	נְגַשְׁתֶּן	נְפַלְתֶּן	נִגַּשְׁתֶּן	נִגַּשְׁתֶּן	נֻגַּשְׁתֶּן
1 c.p.	נָגַשְׁנוּ	נָפַלְנוּ	נִגַּשְׁנוּ	נִגַּשְׁנוּ	נֻגַּשְׁנוּ
Imperfect					
3 m.s.	יִגַּשׁ	יִפֹּל	יִנָּגֵשׁ	יְנַגֵּשׁ	יְנֻגַּשׁ
3 f.s.	תִּגַּשׁ	תִּפֹּל	תִּנָּגֵשׁ	תְּנַגֵּשׁ	תְּנֻגַּשׁ
2 m.s.	תִּגַּשׁ	תִּפֹּל	תִּנָּגֵשׁ	תְּנַגֵּשׁ	תְּנֻגַּשׁ
2 f.s.	תִּגְּשִׁי	תִּפְּלִי	תִּנָּגְשִׁי	תְּנַגְּשִׁי	תְּנֻגְּשִׁי
1 c.s.	אֶגַּשׁ	אֶפֹּל	אֶנָּגֵשׁ	אֲנַגֵּשׁ	אֲנֻגַּשׁ
3 m.p.	יִגְּשׁוּ	יִפְּלוּ	יִנָּגְשׁוּ	יְנַגְּשׁוּ	יְנֻגְּשׁוּ
3 f.p.	תִּגַּשְׁנָה	תִּפֹּלְנָה	תִּנָּגַשְׁנָה	תְּנַגֵּשְׁנָה	תְּנֻגַּשְׁנָה
2 m.p.	תִּגְּשׁוּ	תִּפְּלוּ	תִּנָּגְשׁוּ	תְּנַגְּשׁוּ	תְּנֻגְּשׁוּ
2 f.p.	תִּגַּשְׁנָה	תִּפֹּלְנָה	תִּנָּגַשְׁנָה	תְּנַגֵּשְׁנָה	תְּנֻגַּשְׁנָה
1 c.p.	נִגַּשׁ	נִפֹּל	נִנָּגֵשׁ	נְנַגֵּשׁ	נְנֻגַּשׁ
Imperative					
2 m.s.	גַּשׁ	נְפֹל	הִנָּגֵשׁ	נַגֵּשׁ	
2 f.s.	גְּשִׁי	נִפְלִי	הִנָּגְשִׁי	נַגְּשִׁי	
2 m.p.	גְּשׁוּ	נִפְלוּ	הִנָּגְשׁוּ	נַגְּשׁוּ	
2 f.p.	גַּשְׁנָה	נְפֹלְנָה	הִנָּגַשְׁנָה	נַגֵּשְׁנָה	
Infinitive					
Absolute	נָגוֹשׁ	נָפוֹל	הִנָּגֵשׁ	נַגֵּשׁ	נֻגֹּשׁ
Construct	גֶּשֶׁת	נְפֹל	הִנָּגֵשׁ	נַגֵּשׁ	נֻגַּשׁ
Participle					
Active	נֹגֵשׁ	נֹפֵל		מְנַגֵּשׁ	
Passive	נָגוּשׁ	נָפוּל	נִגָּשׁ		מְנֻגָּשׁ
Imperfect ו consecut.	וַיִּגַּשׁ	וַיִּפֹּל	וַיִּנָּגֶשׁ	וַיְנַגֵּשׁ	וַיְנֻגַּשׁ
Jussive	יִגַּשׁ	יִפֹּל	יִנָּגֶשׁ	יְנַגֵּשׁ	יְנֻגַּשׁ
Cohortative	אֶגְּשָׁה	אֶפְּלָה	אֶנָּגְשָׁה	אֲנַגְּשָׁה	

Refer to §55.

Hitpa'ēl	Hip'îl	Hop'al	Qal נתן	Qal לקח
הִתְנַגֵּשׁ	הִגִּישׁ	הֻגַּשׁ	נָתַן	לָקַח
הִתְנַגְּשָׁה	הִגִּישָׁה	הֻגְּשָׁה	נָתְנָה	לָקְחָה
הִתְנַגַּשְׁתָּ	הִגַּשְׁתָּ	הֻגַּשְׁתָּ	נָתַתָּה	לָקַחְתָּ
הִתְנַגַּשְׁתְּ	הִגַּשְׁתְּ	הֻגַּשְׁתְּ	נָתַתְּ	לָקַחַתְּ
הִתְנַגַּשְׁתִּי	הִגַּשְׁתִּי	הֻגַּשְׁתִּי	נָתַתִּי	לָקַחְתִּי
הִתְנַגְּשׁוּ	הִגִּישׁוּ	הֻגְּשׁוּ	נָתְנוּ	לָקְחוּ
הִתְנַגַּשְׁתֶּם	הִגַּשְׁתֶּם	הֻגַּשְׁתֶּם	נְתַתֶּם	לְקַחְתֶּם
הִתְנַגַּשְׁתֶּן	הִגַּשְׁתֶּן	הֻגַּשְׁתֶּן	נְתַתֶּן	לְקַחְתֶּן
הִתְנַגַּשְׁנוּ	הִגַּשְׁנוּ	הֻגַּשְׁנוּ	נָתַנּוּ	לָקַחְנוּ
יִתְנַגֵּשׁ	יַגִּישׁ	יֻגַּשׁ	יִתֵּן	יִקַּח
תִּתְנַגֵּשׁ	תַּגִּישׁ	תֻּגַּשׁ	תִּתֵּן	תִּקַּח
תִּתְנַגֵּשׁ	תַּגִּישׁ	תֻּגַּשׁ	תִּתֵּן	תִּקַּח
תִּתְנַגְּשִׁי	תַּגִּישִׁי	תֻּגְּשִׁי	תִּתְּנִי	תִּקְחִי
אֶתְנַגֵּשׁ	אַגִּישׁ	אֻגַּשׁ	אֶתֵּן	אֶקַּח
יִתְנַגְּשׁוּ	יַגִּישׁוּ	יֻגְּשׁוּ	יִתְּנוּ	יִקְחוּ
תִּתְנַגֵּשְׁנָה	תַּגֵּשְׁנָה	תֻּגַּשְׁנָה	תִּתֵּנָּה	תִּקַּחְנָה
תִּתְנַגְּשׁוּ	תַּגִּישׁוּ	תֻּגְּשׁוּ	תִּתְּנוּ	תִּקְחוּ
תִּתְנַגֵּשְׁנָה	תַּגֵּשְׁנָה	תֻּגַּשְׁנָה	תִּתֵּנָּה	תִּקַּחְנָה
נִתְנַגֵּשׁ	נַגִּישׁ	נֻגַּשׁ	נִתֵּן	נִקַּח
הִתְנַגֵּשׁ	הַגֵּשׁ		תֵּן	קַח
הִתְנַגְּשִׁי	הַגִּישִׁי		תְּנִי	קְחִי
הִתְנַגְּשׁוּ	הַגִּישׁוּ		תְּנוּ	קְחוּ
הִתְנַגֵּשְׁנָה	הַגֵּשְׁנָה		תֵּנָּה	קַחְנָה
הִתְנַגֵּשׁ	הַגֵּשׁ	הֻגֵּשׁ	נָתוֹן	לָקוֹחַ
הִתְנַגֵּשׁ	הַגִּישׁ	הֻגַּשׁ	תֵּת	קַחַת
מִתְנַגֵּשׁ	מַגִּישׁ		נֹתֵן	לֹקֵחַ
		מֻגָּשׁ	נָתוּן	לָקוּחַ
וַיִּתְנַגֵּשׁ	וַיַּגֵּשׁ	וַיֻּגַּשׁ	וַיִּתֵּן	וַיִּקַּח
יִתְנַגֵּשׁ	יַגֵּשׁ	יֻגַּשׁ	יִתֵּן	יִקַּח
אֶתְנַגְּשָׁה	אַגִּישָׁה		אֶתְּנָה	אֶקְחָה

	Qal	Nip‘al	Pôlēl	Pôlal
Perfect				
3 m.s.	קָם	נָקוֹם	קוֹמֵם	קוֹמַם
3 f.s.	קָמָה	נָקוֹמָה	קוֹמְמָה	קוֹמְמָה
2 m.s.	קַמְתָּ	נְקוּמוֹתָ	קוֹמַמְתָּ	קוֹמַמְתָּ
2 f.s.	קַמְתְּ	נְקוּמוֹת	קוֹמַמְתְּ	קוֹמַמְתְּ
1 c.s.	קַמְתִּי	נְקוּמוֹתִי	קוֹמַמְתִּי	קוֹמַמְתִּי
3 c.p.	קָמוּ	נָקוֹמוּ	קוֹמְמוּ	קוֹמְמוּ
2 m.p.	קַמְתֶּם	נְקוֹמוֹתֶם	קוֹמַמְתֶּם	קוֹמַמְתֶּם
2 f.p.	קַמְתֶּן	נְקוֹמוֹתֶן	קוֹמַמְתֶּן	קוֹמַמְתֶּן
1 c.p.	קַמְנוּ	נְקוּמוֹנוּ	קוֹמַמְנוּ	קוֹמַמְנוּ
Imperfect				
3 m.s.	יָקוּם	יִקּוֹם	יְקוֹמֵם	יְקוֹמַם
3 f.s.	תָּקוּם	תִּקּוֹם	תְּקוֹמֵם	תְּקוֹמַם
2 m.s.	תָּקוּם	תִּקּוֹם	תְּקוֹמֵם	תְּקוֹמַם
2 f.s.	תָּקוּמִי	תִּקּוֹמִי	תְּקוֹמְמִי	תְּקוֹמְמִי
1 c.s.	אָקוּם	אֶקּוֹם	אֲקוֹמֵם	אֲקוֹמַם
3 m.p.	יָקוּמוּ	יִקּוֹמוּ	יְקוֹמְמוּ	יְקוֹמְמוּ
3 f.p.	תְּקוּמֶינָה	תִּקּוֹמְנָה	תְּקוֹמֵמְנָה	תְּקוֹמַמְנָה
2 m.p.	תָּקוּמוּ	תִּקּוֹמוּ	תְּקוֹמְמוּ	תְּקוֹמְמוּ
2 f.p.	תְּקוּמֶינָה	תִּקּוֹמְנָה	תְּקוֹמֵמְנָה	תְּקוֹמַמְנָה
1 c.p.	נָקוּם	נִקּוֹם	נְקוֹמֵם	נְקוֹמַם
Imperative				
2 m.s.	קוּם	הִקּוֹם	קוֹמֵם	
2 f.s.	קוּמִי	הִקּוֹמִי	קוֹמְמִי	
2 m.p.	קוּמוּ	הִקּוֹמוּ	קוֹמְמוּ	
2 f.p.	קֹמְנָה	הִקּוֹמְנָה	קוֹמֵמְנָה	
Infinitive				
Absolute	קוֹם	הִקּוֹם	קוֹמֵם	קוֹמַם
Construct	קוּם	הִקּוֹם	קוֹמֵם	קוֹמַם
Participle				
Active	קָם		מְקוֹמֵם	
Passive	קוּם	נָקוֹם		מְקוֹמָם
Imperfect ו consecut.	וַיָּקָם	וַיִּקּוֹם	וַיְקוֹמֵם	וַיְקוֹמַם
Jussive	יָקֹם	יִקּוֹם	יְקוֹמֵם	יְקוֹמַם
Cohortative	אָקוּמָה	אֶקּוֹמָה	אֲקוֹמְמָה	

Refer to §56.

Hitpôlēl	Hip'îl	Hop'al	Stative Qal	
הִתְקוֹמֵם	הֵקִים	הוּקַם	מֵת	בּוֹשׁ
הִתְקוֹמְמָה	הֵקִימָה	הוּקְמָה	מֵתָה	בּוֹשָׁה
הִתְקוֹמַמְתָּ	הֲקִימוֹתָ	הוּקַמְתָּ	מַתָּה	בֹּשְׁתָּ
הִתְקוֹמַמְתְּ	הֲקִימוֹת	הוּקַמְתְּ	מַתְּ	בֹּשְׁתְּ
הִתְקוֹמַמְתִּי	הֲקִימוֹתִי	הוּקַמְתִּי	מַתִּי	בֹּשְׁתִּי
הִתְקוֹמְמוּ	הֵקִימוּ	הוּקְמוּ	מֵתוּ	בּוֹשׁוּ
הִתְקוֹמַמְתֶּם	הֲקִימוֹתֶם	הוּקַמְתֶּם	מַתֶּם	בָּשְׁתֶּם
הִתְקוֹמַמְתֶּן	הֲקִימוֹתֶן	הוּקַמְתֶּן	מַתֶּן	בָּשְׁתֶּן
הִתְקוֹמַמְנוּ	הֲקִימוֹנוּ	הוּקַמְנוּ	מַתְנוּ	בֹּשְׁנוּ
יִתְקוֹמֵם	יָקִים	יוּקַם	יָמוּת	יֵבוֹשׁ
תִּתְקוֹמֵם	תָּקִים	תּוּקַם	תָּמוּת	תֵּבוֹשׁ
תִּתְקוֹמֵם	תָּקִים	תּוּקַם	תָּמוּת	תֵּבוֹשׁ
תִּתְקוֹמְמִי	תָּקִימִי	תּוּקְמִי	תָּמוּתִי	תֵּבוֹשִׁי
אֶתְקוֹמֵם	אָקִים	אוּקַם	אָמוּת	אֵבוֹשׁ
יִתְקוֹמְמוּ	יָקִימוּ	יוּקְמוּ	יָמוּתוּ	יֵבוֹשׁוּ
תִּתְקוֹמֵמְנָה	תָּקֵמְנָה	תּוּקַמְנָה	תְּמוּתֶינָה	תֵּבֹשְׁנָה
תִּתְקוֹמְמוּ	תָּקִימוּ	תּוּקְמוּ	תָּמוּתוּ	תֵּבוֹשׁוּ
תִּתְקוֹמֵמְנָה	תָּקֵמְנָה	תּוּקַמְנָה	תְּמוּתֶינָה	תֵּבֹשְׁנָה
נִתְקוֹמֵם	נָקִים	נוּקַם	נָמוּת	נֵבוֹשׁ
הִתְקוֹמֵם	הָקֵם		מוּת	בּוֹשׁ
הִתְקוֹמְמִי	הָקִימִי		מוּתִי	בּוֹשִׁי
הִתְקוֹמְמוּ	הָקִימוּ		מוּתוּ	בּוֹשׁוּ
הִתְקוֹמֵמְנָה	הָקֵמְנָה		מֹתְנָה	בֹּשְׁנָה
הִתְקוֹמֵם	הָקֵם	הוּקֵם	מוֹת	בּוֹשׁ
הִתְקוֹמֵם	הָקִים	הוּקַם	מוּת	בּוֹשׁ
מִתְקוֹמֵם	מֵקִים		מֵת	בּוֹשׁ
		מוּקָם		
וַיִּתְקוֹמֵם	וַיָּקֶם	וַיּוּקַם	וַיָּמֶת	וַיֵּבֹשׁ
יִתְקוֹמֵם	יָקֵם	יוּקַם	יָמֵת	יֵבֹשׁ
אֶתְקוֹמְמָה	אָקִימָה		אָמוּתָה	אֵבוֹשָׁה

	Qal	Nipʿal	Pôlēl
Perfect			
3 m.s.	בָּן		
3 f.s.	בָּנָה		
2 m.s.	בַּנְתָּ		
2 f.s.	בַּנְתְּ		
1 c.s.	בַּנְתִּי		
3 c.p.	בָּנוּ		
2 m.p.	בַּנְתֶּם		
2 f.p.	בַּנְתֶּן		
1 c.p.	בַּנּוּ		
Imperfect			
3 m.s.	יָבִין		
3 f.s.	תָּבִין		
2 m.s.	תָּבִין		
2 f.s.	תָּבִינִי		
1 c.s.	אָבִין		
3 m.p.	יָבִינוּ		
3 f.p.	תְּבִינֶינָה		
2 m.p.	תָּבִינוּ		
2 f.p.	תְּבִינֶינָה		
1 c.p.	נָבִין		
Imperative			
2 m.s.	בִּין		
2 f.s.	בִּינִי		
2 m.p.	בִּינוּ		
2 f.p.	בֵּנָּה		
Infinitive			
Absolute	בּוֹן		
Construct	בִּין		
Participle			
Active	בָּן		
Passive	בִּין		
Imperfect ו consecut.	וַיָּבֶן		
Jussive	יָבֵן		
Cohortative	אָבִינָה		

Refer to §56. With the exception of some forms of Qal, the conjugation of the ע"י verb is

Pôlal	Hiṯp̱ôlēl	Hip̱ʻîl	Hop̱ʻal	
				Perfect 3 m.s. 3 f.s. 2 m.s. 2 f.s. 1 c.s. 3 c.p. 2 m.p. 2 f.p. 1 c.p.
				Imperfect 3 m.s. 3 f.s. 2 m.s. 2 f.s. 1 c.s. 3 m.p. 3 f.p. 2 m.p. 2 f.p. 1 c.p.
				Imperative 2 m.s. 2 f.s. 2 m.p. 2 f.p.
				Infinitive Absolute Construct
				Participle Active Passive
				Imperfect ו consecut.
				Jussive
				Cohortative

like the ע"ו verb.

	Qal	Nipʻal	Pôlēl
Perfect 3 m.s.	סַב	נָסַב	סוֹבֵב
3 f.s.	סָֽבָּה	נָֽסַבָּה	סֽוֹבְבָה
2 m.s.	סַבּ֫וֹתָ	נְסַבּ֫וֹתָ	סוֹבַ֫בְתָּ
2 f.s.	סַבּוֹת	נְסַבּוֹת	סוֹבַבְתְּ
1 c.s.	סַבּ֫וֹתִי	נְסַבּ֫וֹתִי	סוֹבַ֫בְתִּי
3 c.p.	סַ֫בּוּ	נָסַ֫בּוּ	סֽוֹבְבוּ
2 m.p.	סַבּוֹתֶם	נְסַבּוֹתֶם	סֽוֹבַבְתֶּם
2 f.p.	סַבּוֹתֶן	נְסַבּוֹתֶן	סֽוֹבַבְתֶּן
1 c.p.	סַבּ֫וֹנוּ	נְסַבּ֫וֹנוּ	סוֹבַ֫בְנוּ
Imperfect 3 m.s.	יִסֹּב יָסֹב	יִסַּב	יְסוֹבֵב
3 f.s.	תִּסֹּב תָּסֹב	תִּסַּב	תְּסוֹבֵב
2 m.s.	תִּסֹּב תָּסֹב	תִּסַּב	תְּסוֹבֵב
2 f.s.	תִּסֹּ֫בִּי תָּסֹ֫בִּי	תִּסַּ֫בִּי	תְּסֽוֹבְבִי
1 c.s.	אֶסֹּב אָסֹב	אֶסַּב	אֲסוֹבֵב
3 m.p.	יִסֹּ֫בּוּ יָסֹ֫בּוּ	יִסַּ֫בּוּ	יְסֽוֹבְבוּ
3 f.p.	תִּסֹּ֫בְנָה תְּסֻבֶּ֫ינָה	תִּסַּבֶּ֫ינָה	תְּסוֹבֵ֫בְנָה
2 m.p.	תִּסֹּ֫בּוּ תָּסֹ֫בּוּ	תִּסַּ֫בּוּ	תְּסֽוֹבְבוּ
2 f.p.	תִּסֹּ֫בְנָה תְּסֻבֶּ֫ינָה	תִּסַּבֶּ֫ינָה	תְּסוֹבֵ֫בְנָה
1 c.p.	נִסֹּב נָסֹב	נִסַּב	נְסוֹבֵב
Imperative 2 m.s.	סֹב	הִסַּב	סוֹבֵב
2 f.s.	סֹ֫בִּי	הִסַּ֫בִּי	סֽוֹבְבִי
2 m.p.	סֹ֫בּוּ	הִסַּ֫בּוּ	סֽוֹבְבוּ
2 f.p.	סֻבֶּ֫ינָה	הִסַּבֶּ֫ינָה	סוֹבֵ֫בְנָה
Infinitive Absolute	סָבוֹב	הִסֹּב	סוֹבֵב
Construct	סֹב	הִסַּב	סוֹבֵב
Participle Active	סוֹבֵג		מְסוֹבֵב
Passive	סָבוּב	נָסָב	
Imperfect ו consecut.	וַיִּסֹּב וַיָּ֫סָב	וַיִּסַּב	וַיְסוֹבֵב
Jussive	יִסֹּב יָסֹב	יִסַּב	יְסוֹבֵב
Cohortative	אֶסֹּ֫בָּה אָסֹ֫בָּה	אֶסַּ֫בָּה	אֲסֽוֹבְבָה

Refer to §57.

Pôlal	Hitp̱ôlēl	Hip̱'îl	Hop̱'al
סוֹבַב סֹוֹבְבָה סוֹבַבְתָּ סוֹבַבְתְּ סוֹבַבְתִּי סוֹבְבוּ סוֹבַבְתֶּם סוֹבַבְתֶּן סוֹבַבְנוּ	הִסְתּוֹבֵב הִסְתּוֹבְבָה הִסְתּוֹבַבְתָּ הִסְתּוֹבַבְתְּ הִסְתּוֹבַבְתִּי הִסְתּוֹבְבוּ הִסְתּוֹבַבְתֶּם הִסְתּוֹבַבְתֶּן הִסְתּוֹבַבְנוּ	הֵסֵב הֵסַבָּה הֲסִבּוֹתָ הֲסִבּוֹת הֲסִבּוֹתִי הֵסַבּוּ הֲסִבּוֹתֶם הֲסִבּוֹתֶן הֲסִבּוֹנוּ	הוּסַב הוּסַבָּה הוּסַבּוֹתָ הוּסַבּוֹת הוּסַבּוֹתִי הוּסַבּוּ הוּסַבּוֹתֶם הוּסַבּוֹתֶן הוּסַבּוֹנוּ
יְסוֹבַב תְּסוֹבַב תְּסוֹבַב תְּסוֹבְבִי אֲסוֹבַב יְסוֹבְבוּ תְּסוֹבַבְנָה תְּסוֹבְבוּ תְּסוֹבַבְנָה נְסוֹבַב	יִסְתּוֹבֵב תִּסְתּוֹבֵב תִּסְתּוֹבֵב תִּסְתּוֹבְבִי אֶסְתּוֹבֵב יִסְתּוֹבְבוּ תִּסְתּוֹבֵבְנָה תִּסְתּוֹבְבוּ תִּסְתּוֹבֵבְנָה נִסְתּוֹבֵב	יָסֵב תָּסֵב תָּסֵב תָּסֵבִּי אָסֵב יָסֵבּוּ תְּסִבֶּינָה תָּסֵבּוּ תְּסִבֶּינָה נָסֵב	יוּסַב תּוּסַב תּוּסַב תּוּסַבִּי אוּסַב יוּסַבּוּ תּוּסַבֶּינָה תּוּסַבּוּ תּוּסַבֶּינָה נוּסַב
	הִסְתּוֹבֵב הִסְתּוֹבְבִי הִסְתּוֹבְבוּ הִסְתּוֹבֵבְנָה	הָסֵב הָסֵבִּי הָסֵבּוּ הֲסִבֶּינָה	
סוֹבַב סוֹבַב	הִסְתּוֹבֵב הִסְתּוֹבֵב	הָסֵב הָסֵב	הוּסֵב הוּסַב
מְסוֹבָב	מִסְתּוֹבֵב	מֵסֵב	מוּסָב
וַיְסוֹבַב	וַיִּסְתּוֹבֵב	וַיָּסֶב	וַיּוּסַב
יְסוֹבַב	יִסְתּוֹבֵב	יָסֵב	יוּסַב
	אֶסְתּוֹבְבָה	אָסֵבָּה	

פ Laryngeal--ל"ה

	Qal	Nip'al	Pi'ēl	Pu'al
Perfect				
3 m.s.	עָשָׂה	נֶעֱשָׂה	עִשָּׂה	עֻשָּׂה
3 f.s.	עָשְׂתָה	נֶעֶשְׂתָה	עִשְּׂתָה	עֻשְּׂתָה
2 m.s.	עָשִׂיתָ	נֶעֱשֵׂיתָ	עִשִּׂיתָ	עֻשֵּׂיתָ
2 f.s.	עָשִׂית	נֶעֱשֵׂית	עִשִּׂית	עֻשֵּׂית
1 c.s.	עָשִׂיתִי	נֶעֱשֵׂיתִי	עִשִּׂיתִי	עֻשֵּׂיתִי
3 c.p.	עָשׂוּ	נֶעֱשׂוּ	עִשּׂוּ	עֻשּׂוּ
2 m.p.	עֲשִׂיתֶם	נֶעֱשֵׂיתֶם	עִשִּׂיתֶם	עֻשֵּׂיתֶם
2 f.p.	עֲשִׂיתֶן	נֶעֱשֵׂיתֶן	עִשִּׂיתֶן	עֻשֵּׂיתֶן
1 c.p.	עָשִׂינוּ	נֶעֱשֵׂינוּ	עִשִּׂינוּ	עֻשֵּׂינוּ
Imperfect				
3 m.s.	יַעֲשֶׂה	יֵעָשֶׂה	יְעַשֶּׂה	יְעֻשֶּׂה
3 f.s.	תַּעֲשֶׂה	תֵּעָשֶׂה	תְּעַשֶּׂה	תְּעֻשֶּׂה
2 m.s.	תַּעֲשֶׂה	תֵּעָשֶׂה	תְּעַשֶּׂה	תְּעֻשֶּׂה
2 f.s.	תַּעֲשִׂי	תֵּעָשִׂי	תְּעַשִּׂי	תְּעֻשִּׂי
1 c.s.	אֶעֱשֶׂה	אֵעָשֶׂה	אֲעַשֶּׂה	אֲעֻשֶּׂה
3 m.p.	יַעֲשׂוּ	יֵעָשׂוּ	יְעַשּׂוּ	יְעֻשּׂוּ
3 f.p.	תַּעֲשֶׂינָה	תֵּעָשֶׂינָה	תְּעַשֶּׂינָה	תְּעֻשֶּׂינָה
2 m.p.	תַּעֲשׂוּ	תֵּעָשׂוּ	תְּעַשּׂוּ	תְּעֻשּׂוּ
2 f.p.	תַּעֲשֶׂינָה	תֵּעָשֶׂינָה	תְּעַשֶּׂינָה	תְּעֻשֶּׂינָה
1 c.p.	נַעֲשֶׂה	נֵעָשֶׂה	נְעַשֶּׂה	נְעֻשֶּׂה
Imperative				
2 m.s.	עֲשֵׂה	הֵעָשֵׂה	עַשֵּׂה	
2 f.s.	עֲשִׂי	הֵעָשִׂי	עַשִּׂי	
2 m.p.	עֲשׂוּ	הֵעָשׂוּ	עַשּׂוּ	
2 f.p.	עֲשֶׂינָה	הֵעָשֶׂינָה	עַשֶּׂינָה	
Infinitive				
Absolute	עָשֹׂה	הֵעָשֹׂה	עַשֹּׂה	עֻשֹּׂה
Construct	עֲשׂוֹת	הֵעָשׂוֹת	עַשּׂוֹת	עֻשּׂוֹת
Participle				
Active	עֹשֶׂה		מְעַשֶּׂה	
Passive	עָשׂוּי	נַעֲשֶׂה		מְעֻשֶּׂה
Imperfect ו consecut.	וַיַּעַשׂ	וַיֵּעָשׂ	וַיְעַשׂ	וַיְעֻשׂ
Jussive	יַעַשׂ	יֵעָשׂ	יְעַשׂ	יְעֻשׂ
Cohortative	See §52.6			

Refer to §§ 48, 52.

Hitpa'ēl	Hip'îl	Hop'al	
			Perfect
הִתְעַשָּׂה	הֶעֱשָׂה	הָעֳשָׂה	3 m.s.
הִתְעַשְּׂתָה	הֶעֶשְׂתָה	הָעָשְׂתָה	3 f.s.
הִתְעַשִּׂיתָ	הֶעֱשִׂיתָ	הָעֳשֵׂיתָ	2 m.s.
הִתְעַשִּׂית	הֶעֱשִׂית	הָעֳשֵׂית	2 f.s.
הִתְעַשִּׂיתִי	הֶעֱשִׂיתִי	הָעֳשֵׂיתִי	1 c.s.
הִתְעַשּׂוּ	הֶעֱשׂוּ	הָעֳשׂוּ	3 c.p.
הִתְעַשִּׂיתֶם	הֶעֱשִׂיתֶם	הָעֳשֵׂיתֶם	2 m.p.
הִתְעַשִּׂיתֶן	הֶעֱשִׂיתֶן	הָעֳשֵׂיתֶן	2 f.p.
הִתְעַשִּׂינוּ	הֶעֱשִׂינוּ	הָעֳשֵׂינוּ	1 c.p.
			Imperfect
יִתְעַשֶּׂה	יַעֲשֶׂה	יָעֳשֶׂה	3 m.s.
תִּתְעַשֶּׂה	תַּעֲשֶׂה	תָּעֳשֶׂה	3 f.s.
תִּתְעַשֶּׂה	תַּעֲשֶׂה	תָּעֳשֶׂה	2 m.s.
תִּתְעַשִּׂי	תַּעֲשִׂי	תָּעֳשִׂי	2 f.s.
אֶתְעַשֶּׂה	אַעֲשֶׂה	אָעֳשֶׂה	1 c.s.
יִתְעַשּׂוּ	יַעֲשׂוּ	יָעֳשׂוּ	3 m.p.
תִּתְעַשֶּׂינָה	תַּעֲשֶׂינָה	תָּעֳשֶׂינָה	3 f.p.
תִּתְעַשּׂוּ	תַּעֲשׂוּ	תָּעֳשׂוּ	2 m.p.
תִּתְעַשֶּׂינָה	תַּעֲשֶׂינָה	תָּעֳשֶׂינָה	2 f.p.
נִתְעַשֶּׂה	נַעֲשֶׂה	נָעֳשֶׂה	1 c.p.
			Imperative
הִתְעַשֵּׂה	הַעֲשֵׂה		2 m.s.
הִתְעַשִּׂי	הַעֲשִׂי		2 f.s.
הִתְעַשּׂוּ	הַעֲשׂוּ		2 m.p.
הִתְעַשֶּׂינָה	הַעֲשֶׂינָה		2 f.p.
			Infinitive
הִתְעַשֵּׂה	הַעֲשֵׂה	הָעֳשֵׂה	Absolute
הִתְעַשּׂוֹת	הַעֲשׂוֹת	הָעֳשׂוֹת	Construct
			Participle
מִתְעַשֶּׂה	מַעֲשֶׂה		Active
		מָעֳשֶׂה	Passive
וַיִּתְעַשׂ	וַיַּעַשׂ		**Imperfect** ו **consecut.**
יִתְעַשׂ	יַעַשׂ		**Jussive**
			Cohortative

ל"ה--פ"ן

	Qal	Nipʿal	Piʿēl	Puʿal
Perfect				
3 m.s.	נָכָה	נִכָּה	נִכָּה	נֻכָּה
3 f.s.	נָכְתָה	נִכְּתָה	נִכְּתָה	נֻכְּתָה
2 m.s.	נָכִיתָ	נִכֵּיתָ	נִכִּיתָ	נֻכֵּיתָ
2 f.s.	נָכִית	נִכֵּית	נִכִּית	נֻכֵּית
1 c.s.	נָכִיתִי	נִכֵּיתִי	נִכִּיתִי	נֻכֵּיתִי
3 c.p.	נָכוּ	נִכּוּ	נִכּוּ	נֻכּוּ
2 m.p.	נְכִיתֶם	נִכֵּיתֶם	נִכִּיתֶם	נֻכֵּיתֶם
2 f.p.	נְכִיתֶן	נִכֵּיתֶן	נִכִּיתֶן	נֻכֵּיתֶן
1 c.p.	נָכִינוּ	נִכֵּינוּ	נִכִּינוּ	נֻכֵּינוּ
Imperfect				
3 m.s.	יִכֶּה	יִנָּכֶה	יְנַכֶּה	יְנֻכֶּה
3 f.s.	תִּכֶּה	תִּנָּכֶה	תְּנַכֶּה	תְּנֻכֶּה
2 m.s.	תִּכֶּה	תִּנָּכֶה	תְּנַכֶּה	תְּנֻכֶּה
2 f.s.	תִּכִּי	תִּנָּכִי	תְּנַכִּי	תְּנֻכִּי
1 c.s.	אֶכֶּה	אֶנָּכֶה	אֲנַכֶּה	אֲנֻכֶּה
3 m.p.	יִכּוּ	יִנָּכוּ	יְנַכּוּ	יְנֻכּוּ
3 f.p.	תִּכֶּינָה	תִּנָּכֶינָה	תְּנַכֶּינָה	תְּנֻכֶּינָה
2 m.p.	תִּכּוּ	תִּנָּכוּ	תְּנַכּוּ	תְּנֻכּוּ
2 f.p.	תִּכֶּינָה	תִּנָּכֶינָה	תְּנַכֶּינָה	תְּנֻכֶּינָה
1 c.p.	נִכֶּה	נִנָּכֶה	נְנַכֶּה	נְנֻכֶּה
Imperative				
2 m.s.	נְכֵה	הִנָּכֵה	נַכֵּה	
2 f.s.	נְכִי	חִנָּכִי	נַכִּי	
2 m.p.	נְכוּ	הִנָּכוּ	נַכּוּ	
2 f.p.	נְכֶינָה	הִנָּכֶינָה	נַכֶּינָה	
Infinitive				
Absolute	נָכֹה	הִנָּכֹה	נַכֹּה	נֻכֹּה
Construct	נְכוֹת	הִנָּכוֹת	נַכּוֹת	נֻכּוֹת
Participle				
Active	נֹכֶה		מְנַכֶּה	
Passive	נָכוּי	נִכֶּה		מְנֻכֶּה
Imperfect ו consecut.	וַיֵּךְ	וַיִּנָּךְ	וַיְנַךְ	וַיְנֻךְ
Jussive	יֵךְ	יִנָּךְ	יְנַךְ	יְנֻךְ
Cohortative	See §52.6			

Refer to §§ 52, 55.

Hitpaʿēl	Hipʿîl	Hopʿal	
			Perfect
הִתְנַכָּה	הִכָּה	הֻכָּה	3 m.s.
הִתְנַכְּתָה	הִכְּתָה	הֻכְּתָה	3 f.s.
הִתְנַכִּיתָ	הִכִּיתָ	הֻכֵּיתָ	2 m.s.
הִתְנַכִּית	הִכִּית	הֻכֵּית	2 f.s.
הִתְנַכִּיתִי	הִכִּיתִי	הֻכֵּיתִי	1 c.s.
הִתְנַכּוּ	הִכּוּ	הֻכּוּ	3 c.p.
הִתְנַכִּיתֶם	הִכִּיתֶם	הֻכֵּיתֶם	2 m.p.
הִתְנַכִּיתֶן	הִכִּיתֶן	הֻכֵּיתֶן	2 f.p.
הִתְנַכִּינוּ	הִכִּינוּ	הֻכֵּינוּ	1 c.p.
			Imperfect
יִתְנַכֶּה	יַכֶּה	יֻכֶּה	3 m.s.
תִּתְנַכֶּה	תַּכֶּה	תֻּכֶּה	3 f.s.
תִּתְנַכֶּה	תַּכֶּה	תֻּכֶּה	2 m.s.
תִּתְנַכִּי	תַּכִּי	תֻּכִּי	2 f.s.
אֶתְנַכֶּה	אַכֶּה	אֻכֶּה	1 c.s.
יִתְנַכּוּ	יַכּוּ	יֻכּוּ	3 m.p.
תִּתְנַכֶּינָה	תַּכֶּינָה	תֻּכֶּינָה	3 f.p.
תִּתְנַכּוּ	תַּכּוּ	תֻּכּוּ	2 m.p.
תִּתְנַכֶּינָה	תַּכֶּינָה	תֻּכֶּינָה	2 f.p.
נִתְנַכֶּה	נַכֶּה	נֻכֶּה	1 c.p.
			Imperative
הִתְנַכֵּה	הַכֵּה		2 m.s.
הִתְנַכִּי	הַכִּי		2 f.s.
הִתְנַכּוּ	הַכּוּ		2 m.p.
הִתְנַכֶּינָה	הַכֶּינָה		2 f.p.
			Infinitive
הִתְנַכֹּה	הַכֵּה	הֻכֵּה	Absolute
הִתְנַכּוֹת	הַכּוֹת	הֻכּוֹת	Construct
			Participle
מִתְנַכֶּה	מַכֶּה		Active
		מֻכֶּה	Passive
וַיִּתְנַךְ	וַיַּךְ		Imperfect ו consecut.
יִתְנַךְ	יַךְ		Jussive
			Cohortative

ל"א--פ"ן

	Qal	Nip̠'al	Pi'ēl	Pu'al
Perfect				
3 m.s.	נָשָׂא	נִשָּׂא	נִשֵּׂא	נֻשָּׂא
3 f.s.	נָֽשְׂאָה	נִשְּׂאָה	נִשְּׂאָה	נֻשְּׂאָה
2 m.s.	נָשָׂאתָ	נִשֵּׂאתָ	נִשֵּׂאתָ	נֻשֵּׂאתָ
2 f.s.	נָשָׂאת	נִשֵּׂאת	נִשֵּׂאת	נֻשֵּׂאת
1 c.s.	נָשָׂאתִי	נִשֵּׂאתִי	נִשֵּׂאתִי	נֻשֵּׂאתִי
3 c.p.	נָֽשְׂאוּ	נִשְּׂאוּ	נִשְּׂאוּ	נֻשְּׂאוּ
2 m.p.	נְשָׂאתֶם	נִשֵּׂאתֶם	נִשֵּׂאתֶם	נֻשֵּׂאתֶם
2 f.p.	נְשָׂאתֶן	נִשֵּׂאתֶן	נִשֵּׂאתֶן	נֻשֵּׂאתֶן
1 c.p.	נָשָׂאנוּ	נִשֵּׂאנוּ	נִשֵּׂאנוּ	נֻשֵּׂאנוּ
Imperfect				
3 m.s.	יִשָּׂא	יִנָּשֵׂא	יְנַשֵּׂא	יְנֻשָּׂא
3 f.s.	תִּשָּׂא	תִּנָּשֵׂא	תְּנַשֵּׂא	תְּנֻשָּׂא
2 m.s.	תִּשָּׂא	תִּנָּשֵׂא	תְּנַשֵּׂא	תְּנֻשָּׂא
2 f.s.	תִּשְּׂאִי	תִּנָּֽשְׂאִי	תְּנַשְּׂאִי	תְּנֻשְּׂאִי
1 c.s.	אֶשָּׂא	אֶנָּשֵׂא	אֲנַשֵּׂא	אֲנֻשָּׂא
3 m.p.	יִשְּׂאוּ	יִנָּֽשְׂאוּ	יְנַשְּׂאוּ	יְנֻשְּׂאוּ
3 f.p.	תִּשֶּׂאנָה	תִּנָּשֶׂאנָה	תְּנַשֶּׂאנָה	תְּנֻשֶּׂאנָה
2 m.p.	תִּשְּׂאוּ	תִּנָּֽשְׂאוּ	תְּנַשְּׂאוּ	תְּנֻשְּׂאוּ
2 f.p.	תִּשֶּׂאנָה	תִּנָּשֶׂאנָה	תְּנַשֶּׂאנָה	תְּנֻשֶּׂאנָה
1 c.p.	נִשָּׂא	נִנָּשֵׂא	נְנַשֵּׂא	נְנֻשָּׂא
Imperative				
2 m.s.	שָׂא	הִנָּשֵׂא	נַשֵּׂא	
2 f.s.	שְׂאִי	הִנָּֽשְׂאִי	נַשְּׂאִי	
2 m.p.	שְׂאוּ	הִנָּֽשְׂאוּ	נַשְּׂאוּ	
2 f.p.	שֶׂאנָה	הִנָּשֶׂאנָה	נַשֶּׂאנָה	
Infinitive				
Absolute	נָשׂוֹא	הִנָּשֹׂא	נַשֹּׂא	נֻשֹּׂא
Construct	שְׂאֵת	הִנָּשֵׂא	נַשֵּׂא	נֻשָּׂא
Participle				
Active	נֹשֵׂא		מְנַשֵּׂא	
Passive	נָשׂוּא	נִשָּׂא		מְנֻשָּׂא
Imperfect ו consecut.	וַיִּשָּׂא	וַיִּנָּשֵׂא	וַיְנַשֵּׂא	וַיְנֻשָּׂא
Jussive	יִשָּׂא	יִנָּשֵׂא	יְנַשֵּׂא	יְנֻשָּׂא
Cohortative	אֶשְּׂאָה	אֶנָּֽשְׂאָה	אֲנַשְּׂאָה	

Refer to §§ 53, 55.

Hitpa'ēl	Hip'îl	Hop'al	
			Perfect
הִתְנַשֵּׂא	הִשִּׂיא	הֻשָּׂא	3 m.s.
הִתְנַשְּׂאָה	הִשִּׂיאָה	הֻשְּׂאָה	3 f.s.
הִתְנַשֵּׂאתָ	הִשֵּׂאתָ	הֻשֵּׂאתָ	2 m.s.
הִתְנַשֵּׂאת	הִשֵּׂאת	הֻשֵּׂאת	2 f.s.
הִתְנַשֵּׂאתִי	הִשֵּׂאתִי	הֻשֵּׂאתִי	1 c.s.
הִתְנַשְּׂאוּ	הִשִּׂיאוּ	הֻשְּׂאוּ	3 c.p.
הִתְנַשֵּׂאתֶם	הִשֵּׂאתֶם	הֻשֵּׂאתֶם	2 m.p.
הִתְנַשֵּׂאתֶן	הִשֵּׂאתֶן	הֻשֵּׂאתֶן	2 f.p.
הִתְנַשֵּׂאנוּ	הִשֵּׂאנוּ	הֻשֵּׂאנוּ	1 c.p.
			Imperfect
יִתְנַשֵּׂא	יַשִּׂיא	יֻשָּׂא	3 m.s.
תִּתְנַשֵּׂא	תַּשִּׂיא	תֻּשָּׂא	3 f.s.
תִּתְנַשֵּׂא	תַּשִּׂיא	תֻּשָּׂא	2 m.s.
תִּתְנַשְּׂאִי	תַּשִּׂיאִי	תֻּשְּׂאִי	2 f.s.
אֶתְנַשֵּׂא	אַשִּׂיא	אֻשָּׂא	1 c.s.
יִתְנַשְּׂאוּ	יַשִּׂיאוּ	יֻשְּׂאוּ	3 m.p.
תִּתְנַשֶּׂאנָה	תַּשֶּׂאנָה	תֻּשֶּׂאנָה	3 f.p.
תִּתְנַשְּׂאוּ	תַּשִּׂיאוּ	תֻּשְּׂאוּ	2 m.p.
תִּתְנַשֶּׂאנָה	תַּשֶּׂאנָה	תֻּשֶּׂאנָה	2 f.p.
נִתְנַשֵּׂא	נַשִּׂיא	נֻשָּׂא	1 c.p.
			Imperative
הִתְנַשֵּׂא	הַשֵּׂא		2 m.s.
הִתְנַשְּׂאִי	הַשִּׂיאִי		2 f.s.
הִתְנַשְּׂאוּ	הַשִּׂיאוּ		2 m.p.
הִתְנַשֶּׂאנָה	הַשֶּׂאנָה		2 f.p.
			Infinitive
הִתְנַשֵּׂא	הַשֵּׂא	הֻשֵּׂא	Absolute
הִתְנַשֵּׂא	הַשִּׂיא	הֻשָּׂא	Construct
			Participle
מִתְנַשֵּׂא	מַשִּׂיא		Active
		מֻשָּׂא	Passive
וַיִּתְנַשֵּׂא	וַיַּשֵּׂא	וַיֻּשָּׂא	Imperfect ו consecut.
יִתְנַשֵּׂא	יַשֵּׂא	יֻשָּׂא	Jussive
אֶתְנַשְּׂאָה	אַשִּׂיאָה		Cohortative

ל"ה--פ"ו

	Qal	Nip'al	Pi'ēl	Pu'al
Perfect				
3 m.s.	יָדָה	נוֹדָה	יִדָּה	יֻדָּה
3 f.s.	יָֽדְתָה	נוֹדְתָה	יִדְּתָה	יֻדְּתָה
2 m.s.	יָדִיתָ	נוֹדֵיתָ	יִדִּיתָ	יֻדֵּיתָ
2 f.s.	יָדִית	נוֹדֵית	יִדִּית	יֻדֵּית
1 c.s.	יָדִיתִי	נוֹדֵיתִי	יִדִּיתִי	יֻדֵּיתִי
3 c.p.	יָדוּ	נוֹדוּ	יִדּוּ	יֻדּוּ
2 m.p.	יְדִיתֶם	נוֹדֵיתֶם	יִדִּיתֶם	יֻדֵּיתֶם
2 f.p.	יְדִיתֶן	נוֹדֵיתֶן	יִדִּיתֶן	יֻדֵּיתֶן
1 c.p.	יָדִינוּ	נוֹדֵינוּ	יִדִּינוּ	יֻדֵּינוּ
Imperfect				
3 m.s.	יֵדֶה	יִוָּדֶה	יְוַדֶּה	יְוֻדֶּה
3 f.s.	תֵּדֶה	תִּוָּדֶה	תְּוַדֶּה	תְּוֻדֶּה
2 m.s.	תֵּדֶה	תִּוָּדֶה	תְּוַדֶּה	תְּוֻדֶּה
2 f.s.	תֵּדִי	תִּוָּדִי	תְּוַדִּי	תְּוֻדִּי
1 c.s.	אֵדֶה	אֶוָּדֶה	אֲוַדֶּה	אֲוֻדֶּה
3 m.p.	יֵדוּ	יִוָּדוּ	יְוַדּוּ	יְוֻדּוּ
3 f.p.	תֵּדֶינָה	תִּוָּדֶינָה	תְּוַדֶּינָה	תְּוֻדֶּינָה
2 m.p.	תֵּדוּ	תִּוָּדוּ	תְּוַדּוּ	תְּוֻדּוּ
2 f.p.	תֵּדֶינָה	תִּוָּדֶינָה	תְּוַדֶּינָה	תְּוֻדֶּינָה
1 c.p.	נֵדֶה	נִוָּדֶה	נְוַדֶּה	נְוֻדֶּה
Imperative				
2 m.s.	דֵּה	הִוָּדֵה	יַדֵּה	
2 f.s.	דִּי	הִוָּדִי	יַדִּי	
2 m.p.	דּוּ	הִוָּדוּ	יַדּוּ	
2 f.p.	דֶּינָה	הִוָּדֶינָה	יַדֶּינָה	
Infinitive				
Absolute	יָדֹה	הִוָּדֹה	יַדֹּה	יֻדֹּה
Construct	דֵּית	הִוָּדוֹת	יַדּוֹת	יֻדּוֹת
Participle				
Active	יֹדֶה		מְוַדֶּה	
Passive	יָדוּי	נוֹדֶה		מְוֻדֶּה
Imperfect ו consecut.	וַיֵּד	וַיִּוָּד	וַיְוַד	וַיְוֻד
Jussive	יֵד	יִוָּד	יְוַד	יְוֻד
Cohortative	See §52.6			

Refer to §§ 52, 54.

Hitpa‘ēl	Hip‘îl	Hop‘al	
			Perfect
הִתְוַדָּה	הוֹדָה	הוּדָה	3 m.s.
הִתְוַדְּתָה	הוֹדְתָה	הוּדְתָה	3 f.s.
הִתְוַדִּיתָ	הוֹדִיתָ	הוּדֵיתָ	2 m.s.
הִתְוַדִּית	הוֹדִית	הוּדֵית	2 f.s.
הִתְוַדִּיתִי	הוֹדִיתִי	הוּדֵיתִי	1 c.s.
הִתְוַדּוּ	הוֹדוּ	הוּדוּ	3 c.p.
הִתְוַדִּיתֶם	הוֹדִיתֶם	הוּדֵיתֶם	2 m.p.
הִתְוַדִּיתֶן	הוֹדִיתֶן	הוּדֵיתֶן	2 f.p.
הִתְוַדִּינוּ	הוֹדִינוּ	הוּדֵינוּ	1 c.p.
			Imperfect
יִתְוַדֶּה	יוֹדֶה	יוּדֶה	3 m.s.
תִּתְוַדֶּה	תּוֹדֶה	תּוּדֶה	3 f.s.
תִּתְוַדֶּה	תּוֹדֶה	תּוּדֶה	2 m.s.
תִּתְוַדִּי	תּוֹדִי	תּוּדִי	2 f.s.
אֶתְוַדֶּה	אוֹדֶה	אוּדֶה	1 c.s.
יִתְוַדּוּ	יוֹדוּ	יוּדוּ	3 m.p.
תִּתְוַדֶּינָה	תּוֹדֶינָה	תּוּדֶינָה	3 f.p.
תִּתְוַדּוּ	תּוֹדוּ	תּוּדוּ	2 m.p.
תִּתְוַדֶּינָה	תּוֹדֶינָה	תּוּדֶינָה	2 f.p.
נִתְוַדֶּה	נוֹדֶה	נוּדֶה	1 c.p.
			Imperative
הִתְוַדֵּה	הוֹדֵה		2 m.s.
הִתְוַדִּי	הוֹדִי		2 f.s.
הִתְוַדּוּ	הוֹדוּ		2 m.p.
הִתְוַדֶּינָה	הוֹדֶינָה		2 f.p.
			Infinitive
הִתְוַדֹּה	הוֹדֵה	הוּדֵה	Absolute
הִתְוַדּוֹת	הוֹדוֹת	הוּדוֹת	Construct
			Participle
מִתְוַדֶּה	מוֹדֶה		Active
		מוּדֶה	Passive
וַיִּתְוַד	וַיּוֹד		Imperfect ו consecut.
יִתְוַד	יוֹד		Jussive
			Cohortative

	Qal	Nip̄ʻal	Pi.ʻēl	Puʻal
Perfect				
3 m.s.	יָצָא	נוֹצָא	יִצֵּא	יֻצָּא
3 f.s.	יָצְאָה	נוֹצְאָה	יִצְּאָה	יֻצְּאָה
2 m.s.	יָצָאתָ	נוֹצֵאתָ	יִצֵּאתָ	יֻצֵּאתָ
2 f.s.	יָצָאת	נוֹצֵאת	יִצֵּאת	יֻצֵּאת
1 c.s.	יָצָאתִי	נוֹצֵאתִי	יִצֵּאתִי	יֻצֵּאתִי
3 c.p.	יָצְאוּ	נוֹצְאוּ	יִצְּאוּ	יֻצְּאוּ
2 m.p.	יְצָאתֶם	נוֹצֵאתֶם	יִצֵּאתֶם	יֻצֵּאתֶם
2 f.p.	יְצָאתֶן	נוֹצֵאתֶן	יִצֵּאתֶן	יֻצֵּאתֶן
1 c.p.	יָצָאנוּ	נוֹצֵאנוּ	יִצֵּאנוּ	יֻצֵּאנוּ
Imperfect				
3 m.s.	יֵצֵא	יִוָּצֵא	יְיַצֵּא	יְיֻצָּא
3 f.s.	תֵּצֵא	תִּוָּצֵא	תְּיַצֵּא	תְּיֻצָּא
2 m.s.	תֵּצֵא	תִּוָּצֵא	תְּיַצֵּא	תְּיֻצָּא
2 f.s.	תֵּצְאִי	תִּוָּצְאִי	תְּיַצְּאִי	תְּיֻצְּאִי
1 c.s.	אֵצֵא	אֶוָּצֵא	אֲיַצֵּא	אֲיֻצָּא
3 m.p.	יֵצְאוּ	יִוָּצְאוּ	יְיַצְּאוּ	יְיֻצְּאוּ
3 f.p.	תֵּצֶאנָה	תִּוָּצֶאנָה	תְּיַצֶּאנָה	תְּיֻצֶּאנָה
2 m.p.	תֵּצְאוּ	תִּוָּצְאוּ	תְּיַצְּאוּ	תְּיֻצְּאוּ
2 f.p.	תֵּצֶאנָה	תִּוָּצֶאנָה	תְּיַצֶּאנָה	תְּיֻצֶּאנָה
1 c.p.	נֵצֵא	נִוָּצֵא	נְיַצֵּא	נְיֻצָּא
Imperative				
2 m.s.	צֵא	הִוָּצֵא	יַצֵּא	
2 f.s.	צְאִי	הִוָּצְאִי	יַצְּאִי	
2 m.p.	צְאוּ	הִוָּצְאוּ	יַצְּאוּ	
2 f.p.	צֶאנָה	הִוָּצֶאנָה	יַצֶּאנָה	
Infinitive				
Absolute	יָצוֹא	הִוָּצֵא	יַצֵּא	יֻצָּא
Construct	צֵאת	הִוָּצֵא	יַצֵּא	יֻצָּא
Participle				
Active	יֹצֵא		מְיַצֵּא	
Passive	יָצוּא	נוֹצָא		מְיֻצָּא
Imperfect ו consecut.	וַיֵּצֵא	וַיִּוָּצֵא	וַיְיַצֵּא	וַיְיֻצָּא
Jussive	יֵצֵא	יִוָּצֵא	יְיַצֵּא	יְיֻצָּא
Cohortative	אֵצְאָה	אֶוָּצְאָה	אֲיַצְּאָה	

Refer to §§ 53, 54.

Hitpa‘ēl	Hip‘îl	Hop‘al	
			Perfect
הִתְוַצֵּא	הוֹצִיא	הוּצָא	3 m.s.
הִתְוַצְּאָה	הוֹצִיאָה	הוּצְאָה	3 f.s.
הִתְוַצֵּאתָ	הוֹצֵאתָ	הוּצֵאתָ	2 m.s.
הִתְוַצֵּאת	הוֹצֵאת	הוּצֵאת	2 f.s.
הִתְוַצֵּאתִי	הוֹצֵאתִי	הוּצֵאתִי	1 c.s.
הִתְוַצְּאוּ	הוֹצִיאוּ	הוּצְאוּ	3 c.p.
הִתְוַצֵּאתֶם	הוֹצֵאתֶם	הוּצֵאתֶם	2 m.p.
הִתְוַצֵּאתֶן	הוֹצֵאתֶן	הוּצֵאתֶן	2 f.p.
הִתְוַצֵּאנוּ	הוֹצֵאנוּ	הוּצֵאנוּ	1 c.p.
			Imperfect
יִתְוַצֵּא	יוֹצִיא	יוּצָא	3 m.s.
תִּתְוַצֵּא	תּוֹצִיא	תּוּצָא	3 f.s.
תִּתְוַצֵּא	תּוֹצִיא	תּוּצָא	2 m.s.
תִּתְוַצְּאִי	תּוֹצִיאִי	תּוּצְאִי	2 f.s.
אֶתְוַצֵּא	אוֹצִיא	אוּצָא	1 c.s.
יִתְוַצְּאוּ	יוֹצִיאוּ	יוּצְאוּ	3 m.p.
תִּתְוַצֶּאנָה	תּוֹצֶאנָה	תּוּצֶאנָה	3 f.p.
תִּתְוַצְּאוּ	תּוֹצִיאוּ	תּוּצְאוּ	2 m.p.
תִּתְוַצֶּאנָה	תּוֹצֶאנָה	תּוּצֶאנָה	2 f.p.
נִתְוַצֵּא	נוֹצִיא	נוּצָא	1 c.p.
			Imperative
הִתְוַצֵּא	הוֹצֵא		2 m.s.
הִתְוַצְּאִי	הוֹצִיאִי		2 f.s.
הִתְוַצְּאוּ	הוֹצִיאוּ		2 m.p.
הִתְוַצֶּאנָה	הוֹצֶאנָה		2 f.p.
			Infinitive
הִתְוַצֹּא	הוֹצֵא	הוּצֵא	Absolute
הִתְוַצֵּא	הוֹצִיא	הוּצָא	Construct
			Participle
מִתְוַצֵּא	מוֹצִיא		Active
		מוּצָא	Passive
וַיִּתְוַצֵּא	וַיּוֹצֵא	וַיּוּצָא	Imperfect consecut.
יִתְוַצֵּא	יוֹצֵא	יוּצָא	Jussive
אֶתְוַצְּאָה	אוֹצִיאָה		Cohortative

Recognition of Strong Verb Forms

1 מְדַבֵּר הִמְלַכְתִּי תִּקְדַּשְׁנָה תִּקְרְבִי דִּבַּרְנוּ מָשַׁלְתִּי מְקֻדָּשׁ

2 הָשְׁבַּרְתִּי תִּכְשְׁלוּ תַּשְׂכִּילוּ לִמַּדְתִּי לָבַשְׁתְּ מָפְקָד יִשָּׁבֵר

3 נִרְדֹּף נַזְכִּיר לְמַדְתֶּם כָּרְתוּ מִתְקַדֵּשׁ יְקַדְּשׁוּ תִּזְכֹּרְנָה

4 רִדַּף נָתְנָה הִנָּתֹן תְּדַבֵּר תִּמְשְׁלִי תִּשָּׁמַרְנָה הָפְקַדְתִּי

5 גְּדַלְתֶּם הַשְׁכֵּם תְּכֻפַּר יִלְבְּשׁוּ יִנָּתֵן קְבַרְתֶּן נִשְׁבַּתְנוּ

6 בַּקְּשִׁי תְּקֻדְּשׁוּ שִׁמְרוּ נִכְרֵת שְׁמַרְתֶּן פָּקַדְנוּ הִכָּרֵת

7 יִסַּגְּרוּ מֹשֵׁל אֶשָּׁבֵר הִמְשִׁילָה מֻשְׁלָה דַּבֹּר יָפְקְדוּ כָּתוּב

8 אֶתְדַּבֵּר הִתְקַדְּשָׁה כָּתַבְתְּ יַזְכִּירוּ הִתְקַדֵּשׁ צְדֹק יְסַפְּרוּ

9 הִצְדַּקְנוּ יִמְלֹךְ הַכְרִית תִּתְקַדְּשׁוּ קְבֹר נִלְבַּשׁ סִפַּרְתָּ

10 אֶלְמַד הָסְגַּר אַקְרִיב סִפֹּרְנָה יִמָּלֵט כַּשֵּׁל יִפְקֹד תַּזְכֵּרְנָה

11 זָכוֹר מַשְׂכִּיר הִכְשַׁלְתָּ תִּכְתֹּב נִלְמַד מָשְׁלִי דַּבֵּר הִזְכַּרְתִּי

12 תִּזְכְּרִי יִמָּכֵר הִמְשִׁילוּ נִמְלָט נִזְכַּרְנוּ אֶכְשֹׁל יִלְבַּשׁ

13 שִׁמַּרְתָּ נִשְׁבָּר נִשְׁמְרָה יִסְפְּרוּ יְקֻדְּשׁוּ גִּדְּלָה

Recognition of Verbs, Infinitives, and Participles

1 גְּמָלוּנִי הִכְלַמְנוּם רִחַמְתִּים תֹּאמְרוּ יַצִּילוּךָ לְהֵיטִיב

2 הָחֵל יוּמַת תְּכַסִּים אֶזְכְּרֶךָּ לַמְּדֵנִי הַאֲזִינִי הִשְׁמִיעֲךָ

3 גֵּרְשֵׁנִי יַנְחִיל וַתּוֹרֶד וַיֶּגֶל תָּשֹׁב בֹּאֲךָ הוֹדוּ וַיֵּט

4 תֵּעָשׂ נִבְנֵית יִכּוֹן הֲרֵעֹתָה תְּחִלֶּינָה יֵרְדוּ תִּקְחוּ

5 יַחְשְׁבוּ יִלְכְּדָהּ בְּחַנְתִּים תַּאַסְפִי יִגְבְּהוּ תִּתְּנִים גָּלְלוּ

6 וַתָּרָם הֶעֱלֵתָם בְּנֵה הַטּוּ עֲשִׂיתִיו הָקֵל נוֹעִיל יְרֶדֶת

7 לֶדֶת לָתֵת נֹאבְדָה גֹּבַהּ יֵעָזְרוּ הַט וָאֲצַו וַתַּשְׁקֶינָה

8 שָׁמֵנִי נַסֹּנוּ הִתַּמּוֹתִי אֶוָּדַע נְטֹעַ וְאָכְלָה אֲהֵבָתֶךָ

9 שְׂרַפְתֶּם יְלָדַתְנִי וַיְשַׁלְּחֵם וַיַּחְלְמוּ מִשְׁחוּ אֶצָּרְךָ אוֹבִישׁ

10 נָמֹגּוּ צִוִּיתִים תִּירֶאנָה קִוּוּ וַתָּשַׁר תָּנוּחַ וַיִּקְּדוּ

11 אֲיַחֵל אִמְרִי נֵחָמוּ תַּאֲמִינוּ תִּסְמְכֵנִי וַתֹּאכַל לִנְדֹּר

12 הֵילֵל אוּכַל וַיָּמָד נָנוּסָה תְּמִתוּן רָאוּהָ וַתַּעַן צְאִי

13 מֵת וַיָּבֶז נָחֲנִי תָּשִׂימִי תָּלִינוּ הֵמִיתוּ יִתְמוֹדֵד

14 נֵדָעֶנּוּ הַגִּידִי מָאֲסוּ שְׁבָרֵךְ גִּדְּלוּ גֹּרְשׁוּ שָׁכַחַתְּ וַתַּגַּע

15 וַתּוֹצֵא הַלְלוּ תָּפֵר אֲרוֹמֵם אֲנִיחֶנּוּ יָאִירוּ וִיחֻנֶּךָּ

16 וָאִיקַץ נָפְלוֹ יֵאָמֵר תִּשְׂמַח גֵּרַשְׁתִּיהוּ הֶחֱזִיקֵךְ הִפְקַדְתּוֹ

17 לְהִשְׁתַּחֲוֹת הַרְפּוּ תִּמּוֹט וַיָּרָם תָּפֵר מַר וַיֵּלֶד וְלָקַחַתְּ

18 וַתִּפֹּל יַאֲכִילֻהוּ שְׁפָטוּנוּ לַעֲזֹב סַעֲדוּ שְׁבִי נֵדָעֶנּוּ

19 יָחֵל וַיְכַלּוּ וָאֱהִי תִּנָּשְׂאוּ צֵא הֵינִיקִיהוּ וַתִּנָּצֵל

20 הִפַּלְתִּיו יֵאָמֵר וַתִּבְלַעְנָה וַיִּמְאֲסוּ עֲזָרַנִי עֲזַבְנֻהוּ

21 תִּרְאֶינָה הֶחֱיֵיתִי וָאֲצַוֶּה יִרְאוּ עֲלֵה עָנְתָה יָצִיצוּ

22 שַׁשְׁתִּי נַסְתֶּם תַּם יָחֹן שְׁלָחַנִי שְׁפַטְתִּיךָ הִכְבַּדְתִּים

23 אֶעֱזְבֶךָּ אֶעְבְּרָה נִלְחֲמוּ מַגְבִּיהַּ לָקַחַת הוֹדַעְתֶּם סְמַכְתִּיו

24 בֹּרַחַת קְחִי תִּקֹּם תָּאֵר וַיִּמֹּלוּ בֹּשְׁתְּ הַשְׁקִינִי אֲעַלְךָ

25 עֲשִׂיתֶן הַס הֲחָיוֹת רְאוּ אֶעֱשֶׂה לִשְׁתּוֹת וַתָּנַח תְּשׁוּבֶינָה

26 הָבִיאוּ הוּחַל יְמַדֵּד סְמַכְתִּיו כִּפַּרְתָּהוּ תֵּאָמְנוּ תַּחְמֹד

27 יְמָאֲנוּ אֲרַחֲמֵךְ תִּלָּקַח לָרֶדֶת תָּמֹדּוּ גַּלְתִּי אֲזַמֶּרְךָ

28 שַׁלְּחֵנִי הַחֲזִיקִי מְהֵרָה יְרַחֵם לִשְׁמֹעַ וַתֹּאבַדְנָה נְתַתִּיהוּ

29 יַצִּיג יְלָדַתּוּ בְּלָמְדִי אֲלַמֶּדְכֶם נֶחְשַׁבְתִּי וְהַעֲבַדְתִּיךָ

30 בְּחָנֵנִי חֵרַפְתִּי תִּשָּׁכַח וַיְפַתַּח הַךְ יָצָאתָ הִשְׁתַּחֲוִיתֶם

31 הֻכְּתָה וַתִּכְלֶינָה בָּזִיתָ שָׁת וַתָּנַח מוֹת הֲרִימוֹתִי

32 תִּרְדְּפוּנִי יֶאֱהָבֶךָּ הִטָּהֲרוּ יִבְחָרֶךָּ יְדַעְנוּם תֹּאכֵל גִּשְׁתּוֹ

33 אַבִּיטָה נָכוֹנָה הַכּוּם אֲבִיתֶם לְקַחְתֶּן הִשְׁמִירְךָ תִּשְׁמְרֶךָּ

34 דְּרָשׁוּנִי הֲבִיאֹנֻם יַאַסְפֵהוּ רְדֹף וַתְּכַל סְמָכֵנִי וַיִּבְטַח

35 הִפְקַדְתּוֹ אֵלֵד הַמּוֹלִיךְ חָנֵּנִי וָאֵשְׁתְּ תִּישַׁן אִיעָצֵךְ

36 יָבֹזּוּ וַיָּמֶת נֶאֱכַל כִּנְפֹל גָּר חַנּוֹתִי גֹּל יִתְרוֹמֵם

37 נוֹשַׁע וַיְסֹבְבֵנִי הִמְצֵאתִיךָ תִּהְיֶינָה הַרְבָּה תֶּרֶף וַנִּגַּל

38 קִוִּיתֶם עָשְׂךָ אַעֲנֵךְ שָׁמְתָהוּ שַׂמְתּוֹ הֵבֵאתִי מִלֵּאתִי

39 וַיִּשְׁתַּחֲווּ יֹאפוּ נֶעֶשְׂתָה וַיִּגְלוּם הִתְבּוֹנַנְתָּ כּוֹנַנְתָּ

40 תָּסוּרוּ שְׁמַרְתַּנִי גְּמָלְךָ דְּרָשׁוּךָ בִּקַּשְׁתֶּם נַשְׁלִיכֵהוּ יַחֲלֹם

41 תֶּחְדַּל תִּזְעַק שַׁלַּח הַצְלַח לֶאֱכֹל וַאֲמַרְתֶּם וַתֹּאכַל הִשִּׂיגוֹ

42 תִּטָּעֵם לָקוֹחַ תִּתּוֹ וַיְנַשֵּׁק נִצָּב טַעַת נִלְחָמָה יְדַעֲנוּם

43 תֹּאכֵל יִתַּן הִגַּעְתֶּם נִתֵּן נֵלְכָה הֶרְאֵךְ תִּוָּרֵא קְרֶאנָה

44 וַיִּרְדְּפֵהוּ בִּקַּשְׁתִּיהוּ עִבְדוּ לְבַהֲלֵנִי וַיְנַחֵם וַיִּשָּׁבַע

45 לִבְרֹחַ יַכִּירָהּ וַתֵּינֶק זַמּוֹתִי מַדּוֹתֶם שַׁבְתָּ יָנוּר לִינִי

46 יִשְׁתּוּ רָאֲתָה וַיְצַו וַתִּשְׁתַּחֲוֶינָה מִלֵּאנוּ שָׁמְרֵם צְעַקְנָה

47 שְׁמַע מַגְבִּיהַּ אֵימֶינָה הוֹשִׁיעָה יוֹשֵׁב בְּלֶכְתְּךָ יָכָלְתִּי

48 תִּצֹּק קַלּוֹת הֵקַלּוּ שֶׁבֶת יָרוּצוּ הַנַּח יָרֵם מָלֹה בְּכוּ

49 הַכֵּךְ הֶעֱלֵיתָ הָרְאֵיתָ תַּצְמִיחַ לִקַּח בָּאת וַיֵּרֶד נָמַסּוּ

50 תִּירְאִי

Words, Meanings, References to Grammar

Genesis, Chapter 1

1.	בְּרֵאשִׁית=בְּ+רֵאשִׁית	in; beginning §§ 8.1; 13.note; 15.1; 67.3; 70.1; 73.1.b
	בָּרָא	he created §§ 4; 53
	אֱלֹהִים	God §§ 4.note 1; 8.1.c; 12.3.a; 33.3
	הַשָּׁמַיִם=הַ·+שָׁמַיִם	the; heavens §§ 9; 14; 33.4
	וְאֵת=וְ+אֵת	and §17.1; 33.1
	הָאָרֶץ=הָ·+אֶרֶץ	the; earth §§ 12.1; 14.3.note
2.	הָיְתָה (היה)	it was §§ 11.2; 52.2.b
	תֹהוּ	formlessness, nothingness, emptiness, waste §2.note 2
	וָבֹהוּ=וְ+בֹהוּ	and; emptiness, void §§ 17.4; 60
	וְחֹשֶׁךְ=וְ+חֹשֶׁךְ	and; darkness §§ 8.note 3; 60
	עַל־פְּנֵי (פָּנִים)	upon; faces §§ 11.3; 34.2.b; 70.5
	תְהוֹם	deep §2.note 2
	רוּחַ	spirit §§ 6; 34.1.b
	מְרַחֶפֶת (רחף)	moving, hovering, brooding §§ 33.note 2; 39.5; 60; 68.2; 72.3.a
	הַמָּיִם=הַ·+מַיִם	the; waters §12.3.b
3.	וַיֹּאמֶר (אמר)	and he said §§ 32.1; 51.1
	יְהִי (היה)	let there be §§ 31.1; 52.4.note
	אוֹר	light
	וַיְהִי (היה)	and there was §§ 32.1.a.note; 52.4.note
4.	וַיַּרְא (ראה)	and he saw §52.4.c
	אֶת־הָאוֹר	the light §21.1.a
	כִּי	that
	טוֹב	good §41.2
	וַיַּבְדֵּל (בדל)	and he divided §§ 30.1; 32.1.c
	בֵּין	between
	וּבֵין	and between §§ 7; 17.2
	הַחֹשֶׁךְ	the darkness §14.2

5.	וַיִּקְרָא (קרא)	and he called §53.1
	לָאוֹר	see above meaning §15.3
	יוֹם	day
	וְלַחֹשֶׁךְ	see above meaning §§ 15.3; 17
	לָיְלָה	night §12.3.pause
	עֶרֶב	evening §60
	בֹקֶר	morning §60
	אֶחָד	one, first §69
6.	רָקִיעַ	firmament, expanse §6
	בְּתוֹךְ=בְּ+תָּוֶךְ	in; midst §§ 34; 60; 70.1
	וִיהִי (היה)	and let there be §§ 17.2 .note; 31.1; 52.4.note
	מַבְדִּיל (בדל)	division, separation §30.1
7.	וַיַּעַשׂ (עשׂה)	and he made §§ 32.3.note; 52.4.c.3
	אֲשֶׁר	which §§ 45; 73.2.a.2.a
	מִתַּחַת=מִן+תַּחַת	from; under, instead §§ 16.2.a; 70.4
	מֵעַל=מִן+עַל	from; upon §§ 16.2.b; 70.4,5
	כֵּן	thus, so
8.	שֵׁנִי	second §69
9.	יִקָּווּ (קָוָה)	let there be gathered §§ 28; 31; 52.2.a
	מָקוֹם	place §66.1
	וְתֵרָאֶה (ראה)	and let appear §§48.2; 52.1.b
	יַבָּשָׁה	dry land §33.2
10.	וּלְמִקְוֵה=וְ+לְ+מִקְוֶה	and with reference to the gathering 17.2; 34; 63; 66.1
	יַמִּים (יָם)	seas §§ 21.1.a.note; 60.note 3
11.	תַּדְשֵׁא (דשא)	let it put forth §31.1.b.2
	דֶּשֶׁא	grass §60
	עֵשֶׂב	herb §60
	מַזְרִיעַ (זרע)	sowing §§ 6; 30
	עֵץ	tree
	פְּרִי	fruit §60
	עֹשֶׂה	§52.1.d

	לְמִינוֹ=לְ+מִין+וֹ	to its kind, species §§ 15; 36.1
	זַרְעוֹ=זֶרַע+וֹ	its seed §60.note 2
	בוֹ=בְּ+וֹ	in it §§ 38; 73.2.a.2.note
12.	וַתּוֹצֵא (יצא)	and it brought forth §§ 32.1.c; 54.1.c.2
	לְמִינֵהוּ=לְ+מִין+הוּ	§§ 15; 35
13.	שְׁלִישִׁי	third §69.7
14.	מְאֹרֹת (מָאוֹר)	lights §§ 4.note 1; 33.note 4
	בִּרְקִיעַ	§§ 15.2.a; 34
	לְהַבְדִּיל (בדל)	§§ 15; 30.1
	וְהָיוּ (היה)	§32.3.b
	לְאֹתֹת (אוֹת)	for signs §§ 4.note 1; 33.3
	וּלְמוֹעֲדִים (מוֹעֵד)	and for seasons, appointed dates §33.note 3
	וּלְיָמִים (יוֹם)	and for days §37
	וְשָׁנִים (שָׁנָה)	and years §33.note 4
15.	לִמְאוֹרֹת	§§ 15.2.a; 33.note 4
	לְהָאִיר (אוֹר)	to give light §56.2
16.	וַיַּעַשׂ (עשׂה)	§§ 32.1.b; 52.4.c.3
	שְׁנֵי (שְׁנַיִם)	two §§ 69.2.a; 34
	הַגְּדֹלִים (גָּדוֹל)	the great §§ 33.4; 41.1
	הַגָּדֹל	the greater §41.3.a
	לְמֶמְשֶׁלֶת (מֶמְשָׁלָה)	for dominion §§ 33.note 2; 34; 60
	הַקָּטֹן	the smaller §41.3.a
	כּוֹכָב	star
17.	וַיִּתֵּן (נתן)	and he set, placed §§ 55.note 2; 61.note 2
	אֹתָם	them §38
18.	וְלִמְשֹׁל (משׁל)	and to rule §§ 15.2.a; 25.1.b
	וַיַּרְא (ראה)	§§ 32; 52.4.c.1
19.	רְבִיעִי	fourth §69.7
20.	יִשְׁרְצוּ (שׁרץ)	let swarm, teem §8.note 1
	שֶׁרֶץ	swarming things §60
	נֶפֶשׁ	soul §60
	חַיָּה	life §33.2

	עוֹף	fowl, bird
	יְעוֹפֵף (עוּף)	let there fly §56.5
21.	תַּנִּינִם	sea-monsters §4.note 1
	כָּל (כֹּל)	all §§ 3.note 3; 11.2.note; 21.1.a; 34; 42.note 2
	הָרֹמֶשֶׂת (רמשׂ)	the one creeping §§ 25.2.a; 33.note 2; 39.5
	לְמִינֵהֶם	§§ 15; 35
	כָּנָף	wing, winged fowl
22.	וַיְבָרֶךְ (ברךְ)	and he blessed §§ 27.note 2; 32.1.a.note,b; 49.2.a
	לֵאמֹר	§51.2.note 1
	פְּרוּ (פרה)	be fruitful §52.2.a
	וּרְבוּ (רבה)	and multiply §52.2.a
	מלא	to fill
	בַּיַּמִּים	§§ 21.1.a.note; 60.note 3
	יִרֶב (רבה)	§§ 31.1; 52.4.c.3
23.	חֲמִישִׁי	fifth §69.7
24.	תּוֹצֵא (יצא)	§§ 31.1.b.2; 54.1.c.2
	לְמִינָהּ=לְ+מִין+ָהּ	§4, <u>mappîq</u>
	בְּהֵמָה	cattle
	רֶמֶשׂ	creeping things §60
	וְחַיְתוֹ	and wild beast §33.1
25.	חַיַּת (חַיָּה)	life §34.2.c
	אֲדָמָה	ground
26.	נַעֲשֶׂה (עשׂה)	let us make §52.6
	אָדָם	man
	בְּצַלְמֵנוּ=בְּ+צֶלֶם+ֵנוּ	in; image; us §§ 35; 60
	כִּדְמוּתֵנוּ=כְּ+דְּמוּת+ֵנוּ	according to; likeness; us §15.2.a
	וְיִרְדּוּ (רדה)	and let them dominate §52.2.a
	דָּגָה	fish
	הָרֹמֵשׂ	§25.2.a
27.	בְּצַלְמוֹ (צֶלֶם)	§§ 35; 60
	אֹתוֹ	him §38
	זָכָר	male

	נְקֵבָה	female
28.	לָהֶם	to them §38
	וְכִבְשֻׁהָ (כבשׁ)	and subdue ye it §§ 4.note 1; 24.3; 39.3
29.	הִנֵּה	behold
	נָתַתִּי (נתן)	§55.note 2
	לָכֶם	§38
	יִהְיֶה (היה)	§52.4.note
	אָכְלָה	food §3.note 3
30.	יֶרֶק	green plants §60
31.	מְאֹד	exceedingly
	שִׁשִּׁי	sixth §69.7

Chapter 2

1.	וַיְכֻלּוּ (כלה)	and they were completed, finished §52.2.a
	צְבָאָם (צָבָא)	their host §36
2.	וַיְכַל (כלה)	see above §52.4.b
	שְׁבִיעִי	seventh §69.7
	מְלָאכָה	work Gesenius-Kautzsch, §23.c
	שׁבת	to rest
3.	קדשׁ	to hallow, sanctify
	אֹתוֹ	§38
	כִּי	because
	לַעֲשׂוֹת (עשׂה)	§52.1.e
4.	תּוֹלֶדֶת	generation §68.2
	בְּהִבָּרְאָם (ברא)	§§ 39.4.a; 71.2.b
5.	שִׂיחַ	bush, shrub, plant
	שָׂדֶה	field §62
	טֶרֶם	not yet, ere, before that §73.3.a.3
	יִהְיֶה (היה)	§52.4.note
	צמח	to sprout, grow
	לֹא	not §73.3.a.1
	מטר	to rain
	אַיִן	nothing, nought §73.3.a.4

	עבד	to work, serve
6.	אֵד	flood
	עלה	to go up, rise
	שׁקה	to drink
7.	יצר	to form, fashion §54.2.b
	עָפָר	dust
	נפח	to breathe §55
	בְּאַפָּיו (אַף)	in his nostrils §61
	חַיִּים	life
8.	נטע	to plant
	גַּן	garden
	עֵדֶן	Eden
	קֶדֶם	front, east, aforetime
	וַיָּשֶׂם (שִׂים)	and he put, placed, set §56.6
	שָׁם	there
9.	חמד	to desire, be pleasant
	מַרְאֶה	sight §66
	מַאֲכָל	food §66
	דַּעַת	knowledge
	רַע	evil
10.	נָהָר	river
	פרד	to separate
	רֹאשׁ	head §37
11.	שֵׁם	name
	סבב	to surround §57.1
	זָהָב	gold
12.	הַהִוא	§§ 42; 75
	בְּדֹלַח	bdellium
	אֶבֶן	stone
	שֹׁהַם	onyx
13.	שֵׁנִי	second
14.	שְׁלִישִׁי	third
	הלךְ	to go, walk §54.1.a.note
	קִדְמָה	eastward
15.	לקח	to take §55.note 1

וַיַּנִּחֵהוּ (נוּחַ) and he placed him (for dāgēš forte see Gesenius-Kautzsch, §72.ee)

לְעָבְדָהּ (עבד) to work it §39.4

לְשָׁמְרָהּ (שׁמר) to keep it §39.4

16. וַיְצַו (צָוָה) and he commanded §52.4.b

לֵאמֹר §51.2.note 1

אכל to eat §51.2

17. מִמֶּנּוּ §38

אֲכָלְךָ §39.4

מוֹת תָּמוּת (מוּת) you shall surely die §§ 25.1.a; 71.1.c.1.a

18. בַּד separation, alone

אֶעֱשֶׂה §52.6

לוֹ §9.note 3

עֵזֶר helper §60

נֶגֶד opposite, before §60

19. וַיִּצֶר and he formed §4.note 1

וַיָּבֵא (בּוֹא) and he brought §56.6

מַה יִקְרָא §43.1

20. מצא to find

21. נפל to fall

תַּרְדֵּמָה deep sleep §66.2

ישׁן to sleep

וַיִּקַּח §55.note 1

צֵלָע rib

סגר to close

בָּשָׂר flesh

22. בנה to build

אִשָּׁה woman §37

וַיְבִאֶהָ (בּוֹא) §§ 4.note 1; 39.2

23. פַּעַם now

עֶצֶם bone §6C

אִישׁ man §37

24 עַל-כֵּן therefore

עזב to leave, forsake

	אָב	father §37
	אֵם	mother §61
	דבק	to cleave
	אִשְׁתּוֹ	§37
25.	עֲרוּמִּים (עור)	naked (cf. Gesenius-Kautzsch, §93.pp)
	בוֹשׁ	to be ashamed §56.5

Chapter 3

1.	נָחָשׁ	serpent
	עָרוּם (ערם)	crafty
	אַף	also, surely
3.	נגע	to touch
	פֶּן	lest §73.3.a.note
	תְּמֻתוּן (מוּת)	ye shall die (The נוּן is a fuller form of the 2nd and 3rd plural imperfect afformative. It occurs 305 times in the Old Testament, 7 times in Genesis.)
5.	ידע	to know
	פקח	to open
	עַיִן	eye §61
6.	תַּאֲוָה	desire, longing §66.2
	שׂכל	to be wise
	גַּם	also
	עִמָּהּ	with her §60
7.	תפר	to sew together
	עָלֶה	leaf §62
	תְּאֵנָה	fig tree
	חֲגוֹרָה	girdle, apron
8.	שׁמע	to hear
	קוֹל	voice
	חבא	to hide
9.	אַיֶּךָּ (אַי)	where are you? §35
10.	יָרֵא	to fear

	אָנֹכִי	I
11.	מִי	who?
	צָוָה	to command
	לְבִלְתִּי	§73.3.a.5 negative with infinitive construct
12.	עִמָּדִי	with me (equivalent in meaning to עִמִּי)
	הִוא	feminine pronoun §75
13.	מַה־זֹּאת	what is this? §43.1
	נשׁא	to deceive §39.1
14.	ארר	to curse
	גָּחוֹן	belly
	עָפָר	dust
	כָּל־יְמֵי חַיֶּיךָ	all the days of your life §§ 34; 37
15.	אֵיבָה	enmity
	שִׁית	to put, place
	שׁוּף	to bruise §§ 21; 40; 56
	עָקֵב	heel
16.	עִצָּבוֹן	labor, pain, sorrow
	הֵרוֹן	pregnancy
	עֶצֶב	grief, sorrow
	ילד	to give birth, bear
	בֵּן	son
	תְּשׁוּקָה	desire §66.2
17.	עֲבוּר	because
18.	קוֹץ	thorn
	דַּרְדַּר	thistle §65
19.	זֵעָה	sweat
	עַד	until
	שׁוּב	return
20.	אֵם	mother
21.	כְּתֹנֶת	tunic
	עוֹר	skin
	לבשׁ	to clothe
22.	הֵן	behold

	עַתָּה	now
	שׁלח	to send
	עוֹלָם	eternity, forever §63
24.	גרשׁ	to drive out
	שׁכן	to dwell
	לַהַט	flame
	חֶרֶב	sword
	הפך	to turn
	דֶּרֶךְ	way

Chapter 4

1.	הרה	to conceive
	קנה	to acquire, buy, get
2.	יסף	to add
	אָח	brother
	רֹעֶה	shepherd
	צֹאן	sheep, flock
3.	קֵץ	end, limit, extremity
	מִנְחָה	offering
4.	בְּכוֹרָה	first-fruit, first-born
	חֵלֶב	fat
	שׁעה	to look upon, respect, regard
5.	חרה	to burn, glow, kindle wrath
7.	יטב	to be good, do well
	שְׂאֵת	forgiveness
	פֶּתַח	door
	חַטָּאת	sin
	רבץ	to lie down, crouch
8.	הרג	to slay
10.	דָּם	blood
	צעק	to cry out
11.	פצה	to open, utter
	פֶּה	mouth
12.	כֹּחַ	strength
	נוּעַ	to move, tremble, wander
	נוּד	to move to and fro, wander

13.	עָוֺן	affliction, punishment
	נשׂא	to bear
14.	סתר	to hide, conceal
15.	לָכֵן	therefore
	נקם	to take vengeance, punish
	נכה	to smite
16.	ישׁב	to sit, dwell
20.	אֹהֶל	tent
	מִקְנֶה	possession, cattle
21.	תפשׂ	to take hold of, handle
	כִּנּוֹר	harp
	עוּגָב	flute
22.	לטשׁ	to hammer, forge
	חרשׁ	to cut, engrave, plow
	נְחֹשֶׁת	copper, bronze
	בַּרְזֶל	iron
	אָחוֹת	sister
23.	אִמְרָה	word, speech
	פצע	to wound, crush
	פֶּצַע	a wound
	חַבּוּרָה	hurt, wound
25.	שִׁית	to put, place
26.	אָז	then
	חלל	to begin, wound, pierce

Chapter 5

1.	סֵפֶר	book
29.	נחם	to console, comfort

Chapter 6

2.	בחר	to choose, try, prove
3.	דּוּן	to judge, rule, strive
	שׁגג	to err
4.	נְפִיל	giant
	גִּבּוֹר	mighty man, warrior

5.	רַב	great
	יֵצֶר	formation, thought
	מַחֲשָׁבָה	device, thought, reckoning
	לֵב	heart
	רַק	only
7.	מחה	to smite, destroy
9.	צַדִּיק	just, righteous
	תָּמִים	perfect, whole
	דּוֹר	generation
11.	שׁחת	to corrupt, destroy
	חָמָס	violence, wrong
14.	תֵּבָה	ark
	קֵן	room, cell
	כפר	to cover
	חוּץ	street
	כֹּפֶר	pitch
15.	אַמָּה	cubit
	אֹרֶךְ	length
	רֹחַב	breadth
16.	צֹהַר	light, opening for light
	צַד	side
17.	מַבּוּל	flood
	גָּוַע	to perish
18.	קוּם	to establish
	בְּרִית	covenant
21.	אסף	to gather

Chapter 7

1.	בַּיִת	house
2.	טָהוֹר	pure, clean
4.	עוֹד	yet, still
	יְקוּם	whatever exists, living thing
11.	חֹדֶשׁ	month
	בקע	to split, open
	מַעְיָן	fountain, spring
	אֲרֻבָּה	window

12.	גֶּשֶׁם	rain
14.	צִפּוֹר	bird
16.	בַּעַד	behind, through
17.	רום	to rise, be lifted up
18.	גבר	to be mighty, prevail
19.	כסה	to cover, conceal
	גֹּבַהּ	height
	הַר	mountain
21.	חָרָבָה	dry land
23.	שׁאר	to remain

Chapter 8

1.	זכר	to remember
	עבר	to pass over
	שׁכךְ	to decrease, subside
2.	סכר	to close, stop
	כלא	to prevent, restrain
3.	חסר	to want, lack, decrease, diminish
4.	נוּחַ	to rest
6.	חַלּוֹן	window, hole
7.	עֹרֵב	raven
8.	יוֹנָה	dove
	קלל	to be small, diminish
9.	מָנוֹחַ	rest, repose
	רֶגֶל	foot
10.	יחל	to wait
11.	עֵת	time
	זַיִת	olive, olive tree
	טָרָף	something plucked
13.	חרב	to dry up
	סוּר	to remove, depart
19.	מִשְׁפָּחָה	family, kind (to join)
20.	מִזְבֵּחַ	altar
	עֹלָה	offering
21.	רוּחַ	to smell
	רֵיחַ	odor

	נִיחֹחַ	pleasantness, sweetness
	קלל	to curse
	נְעוּרָה	youth
22.	קָצִיר	harvest
	קֹר	cold
	חֹם	heat
	קַיִץ	summer
	חֹרֶף	winter

Chapter 9

2.	מוֹרָא	fear, reverence
	חִתָּה	terror, fear
5.	דרשׁ	to require, ask
6.	שׁפך	to shed
9.	אַחַר	after, behind
11.	כרת	to cut, cut off
13.	קֶשֶׁת	bow
	עָנָן	cloud
14.	ענן	to cover, bring a cloud
19.	נפץ	to people, overspread, be scattered
20.	כֶּרֶם	vineyard
21.	יַיִן	wine
	שׁכר	to be drunk
	גלה	to uncover, be naked
22.	עֶרְוָה	nakedness (ערה to be naked, uncover)
	נגד	to make known
23.	שִׂמְלָה	garment
	שְׁכֶם	shoulder, back
	אֲחֹרַנִּית	backward
24.	יקץ	to awake

Chapter 10

5.	לָשׁוֹן	tongue
9.	צַיִד	chase, hunting
10.	מַמְלָכָה	kingdom, reign

19. גְּבוּל border, edge
25. פלג to divide
30. מוֹשָׁב seat, dwelling

Chapter 11

1. שָׂפָה lip, language
2. נסע to journey
בִּקְעָה valley, plain
3. רֵעֶה neighbor, friend
יהב to give §54.note 3.b
לבן to make brick, white
לְבֵנָה brick
שׂרף to burn
חֵמָר pitch, asphalt
חֹמֶר mortar
4. עִיר city
מִגְדָּל tower
5. ירד to go down
6. עַם people
חלל to begin
בצר to withhold, restrain
זמם to plan, devise
7. בלל to mix, confound
9. חדל to cease, leave off
28. מוֹלֶדֶת birth, nativity
29. בַּת daughter
30. עֲקָרָה barren
31. כַּלָּה daughter-in-law

Chapter 12

4. דבר to speak, command
5. רְכוּשׁ property, goods
רכשׁ to collect, acquire
6. אֵלוֹן oak, terebinth, tree (?)
8. עתק to remove, journey

9.	נֶגֶב	south
10.	רָעָב	famine
	גּוּר	to sojourn
	כָּבֵד	to be heavy
11.	קרב	to be near
	יָפֶה	fair, beautiful
13.	לְמַעַן	to the end that, for the sake of
	בִּגְלַל	for the sake of
15.	הלל	to praise
16.	בָּקָר	oxen
	חֲמוֹר	ass
	שִׁפְחָה	maid-servant
	אָתוֹן	she-ass
	גָּמָל	camel
17.	נגע	to touch
	נֶגַע	plague

Chapter 13

2.	כֶּסֶף	silver
3.	תְּחִלָּה	beginning
6.	יַחְדּוֹ	together
	יָכֹל	to be able
7.	רִיב	strife
8.	אַל	not
	מְרִיבָה	contention
9.	שְׂמאוֹל	left, left hand
	ימן	to turn to the right
10.	כִּכָּר	plain (circle)
12.	אהל	to pitch a tent
14.	צְפוֹנָה	north
16.	מנה	to count

Chapter 14

1.	מֶלֶךְ	king
2.	מִלְחָמָה	war, battle

3.	חבר	to join, unite
	עמק	to be deep
	עֵמֶק	valley
	מֶלַח	salt
4.	מרד	to rebel
6.	מִדְבָּר	wilderness
7.	עַיִן	fountain
	מִשְׁפָּט	judgment
8.	ערך	to arrange, array
10.	בְּאֵר	well, pit
	נוס	to flee, escape
13.	פלט	to escape
	פָּלִיט	fugitive
	בַּעַל	possessor, owner
14.	שׁבה	to make captive, capture
	רִיק	to arm, arrange
	חָנִיךְ	trained men
	רדף	to pursue
15.	חלק	to divide, separate
17.	קרא	to meet
18.	כֹּהֵן	priest
20.	מגן	to deliver, give
23.	חוּט	thread, cord
	שְׂרוֹךְ	latchet, thong
	נַעַל	shoe, sandal
	עשׁר	to become rich
24.	בִּלְעֲדֵי	without, except
	חֵלֶק	portion

Chapter 15

1.	מַחֲזֶה	vision
	מָגֵן	shield
	שָׂכָר	reward
2.	עֲרִירִי	childless
	משׁק	to possess, govern
3.	ירשׁ	to inherit

4.	דָּבָר	word
	מֵעֶה	bowels, loins, intestines
5.	חוּצָה	abroad, without
	נבט	to look
	ספר	to number
	כֹּה	so, thus
6.	אמן	to believe
	חשב	to impute, consider, think
	צְדָקָה	righteousness
9.	עֶגְלָה	calf, heifer
	עֵז	goat
	אַיִל	ram
	תֹּר	turtle-dove
	גּוֹזָל	pigeon
10.	בתר	to divide
11.	עַיִט	bird of prey
	פֶּגֶר	body, carcass
	נשב	to blow
12.	שֶׁמֶשׁ	sun
	אֵימָה	terror, fear
13.	גֵּר	stranger
14.	ענה	to afflict
15.	שָׁלוֹם	peace
	קבר	to bury
	שֵׂיבָה	gray hairs (old age)
16.	הֵנָּה	hither
	שָׁלֵם	to be full
	עָוֹן	iniquity, guilt
17.	עֲלָטָה	darkness
	תַּנּוּר	oven, furnace
	עָשָׁן	smoke
	לַפִּיד	torch, flame
	אֵשׁ	fire
	גזר	to cut, divide
	גֶּזֶר	piece, part

Chapter 16

2.	עצר	to shut, close up
	אוּלַי	perhaps, maybe
4.	קלה	to esteem lightly, despise
	גְּבֶרֶת	mistress
5.	חֵיק	bosom
	שׁפט	to judge
8.	אָנָה	whither
	ברח	to flee
9.	מַלְאָךְ	angel, messenger
12.	פֶּרֶא	wild
13.	הֲלֹם	hither, here

Chapter 17

4.	הָמוֹן	multitude, noise
8.	מָגוּר	sojourning
	אֲחֻזָּה	possession
10.	מוּל	to circumcise
11.	עָרְלָה	foreskin
12.	נֵכָר	stranger
14.	עָרֵל	uncircumcised
	פרר	to break
17.	צחק	to laugh
19.	אֲבָל	certainly, but

Chapter 18

2.	נצב	to set over, stand
	רוּץ	to run
	שׁחה	to bow
4.	מְעַט	little
	רחץ	to wash
	שׁען	to stay, rest
5.	פַּת	morsel, crumb
	סעד	to support, refresh

6.	מהר	to hasten
	סְאָה	measure
	קֶמַח	meal
	סֹלֶת	flour
	לוּשׁ	to knead
	עֻגָה	cake
7.	רַךְ	tender
8.	חֶמְאָה	butter
	חָלָב	milk
11.	זָקֵן	to be old
	אֹרַח	way, manner, path
12.	בלה	to become old, decay, wear out
	עֶדְנָה	pleasure
13.	אֻמְנָם	surely
14.	פלא	to be remote, wonderful
15.	כחשׁ	to deny
16.	שׁקף	to look out, see
18.	עצם	to be powerful, strong
20.	זְעָקָה	cry
21.	כָּלָה	wholly, altogether
23.	נגשׁ	to draw near, approach
	ספה	to destroy
	רָשָׁע	wicked, godless
24.	יֵשׁ	there is
25.	חָלִ֫ילָה	God forbid
27.	יאל	to begin, undertake
	אֵפֶר	ashes

Chapter 19

1.	שַׁעַר	gate
2.	לוּן	to remain overnight, lodge
	שׁכם	to rise early
	רְחֹב	wide space, street
3.	פצר	to cut into, urge, press
	מִשְׁתֶּה	feast

	מַצָּה	unleavened bread
	אפה	to bake
4.	שׁכב	to lie down
6.	דֶּלֶת	door
8.	צֵל	shadow
	קוֹרָה	shelter, roof
9.	הָלְאָה	away, farther, beyond
	רעע	to do evil
	שׁבר	to break, destroy
11.	סַנְוֵרִים	blindness
	לאה	to become weary, exhausted
12.	פֹּה	here, hither
	חָתָן	bridegroom, son-in-law
15.	כְּמוֹ	thus, so, as, like, when
	שַׁחַר	dawn, morning
	אוץ	to press, hasten
16.	מהה	to delay, tarry, wait
	חֶמְלָה	pity, mercy
17.	עמד	to stand
	ספה	to consume, destroy
19.	חֶסֶד	mercy
	דבק	pursue, overtake
20.	מִצְעָר	little, small
21.	הפך	to overthrow
24.	גָּפְרִית	brimstone
26.	נְצִיב	pillar, statue
28.	קִיטוֹר	smoke
	כִּבְשָׁן	oven, furnace
29.	הֲפֵכָה	overthrow, destruction
30.	מְעָרָה	cave
31.	בְּכִירָה	first-born
	צְעִירָה	small, younger
34.	מָחֳרָת	next day, tomorrow
	אֶמֶשׁ	yesterday

Chapter 20

3.	חֲלוֹם	dream
	בְּעֻלָה	mistress
5.	נִקָּיוֹן	cleanness, innocence
6.	חשׂך	to withhold
7.	פלל	to pray
8.	אֹזֶן	ear
11.	רַק	surely
	יִרְאָה	fear
13.	תעה	to wander
16.	אֶלֶף	1000
	כְּסוּת	covering
	יכח	to reprove, dispute
17.	רפא	to heal, cure
	אָמָה	maid-servant
18.	בְּעַד	for the sake of
	רֶחֶם	womb

Chapter 21

7.	מלל	to speak
	ינק	to suckle
8.	גמל	to wean
14.	חֵמֶת	bottle
15.	שׁלך	to cast, throw
16.	הַרְחֵק	far away, far off
	טחה	to stretch
18.	חזק	to hold, seize
20.	קַשָּׁת	archer
23.	שׁבע	to swear
	שׁקר	to lie, deal falsely
	נִין	son, offspring
	נֶכֶד	progeny
25.	אוֹדוֹת	turns, circumstances, causes
	גזל	to take, snatch, rob
28.	כִּבְשָׂה	ewe lamb

30.	עֵד	witness
	חפר	to dig
33.	אֶשֶׁל	tamarisk tree

Chapter 22

1.	נסה	to prove, test
2.	יָחִיד	only one
	אהב	to love
3.	חבשׁ	to bind on, saddle
4.	רָחוֹק	afar, distant
6.	מַאֲכֶלֶת	knife
7.	שֶׂה	sheep, goat, lamb
9.	עקד	to bind
10.	שׁחט	to slay
12.	מְאוּמָה	whatever, something
13.	סְבַךְ	thicket
	קֶרֶן	horn
16.	נְאֻם	oracle, declaration
17.	חוֹל	sand
	אֹיֵב	enemy
18.	עֵקֶב	end, result, because
	פִּילֶגֶשׁ	concubine

Notes on the Pronunciation and Writing of Modern Hebrew

The system of pronunciation used in modern Israel is called the Sephardic; this was the pronunciation used by the Sephardim, Jews of Spain and Portugal. The Ashkenazim, Jews of middle and northern Europe, pronounced Hebrew somewhat differently; their pronunciation, still used by many Jews, is called Ashkenazic.

The following tables are based on the Sephardic; Ashkenazic where it differs from the Sephardic is indicated in the footnotes.

Table 1. Consonants

Printed	Written script	Pronunciation
א	א	Glottal stop
בּ, ב	בּ, ב	b, v
גּ, ג	גּ, ג	g
דּ, ד	דּ, ד	d
ה	ה	h
ו	ו	v
ז	ז	z
ח	ח	ch, as in German 'machen'
ט	ט	t
י	י	y
כּ, כ, ך	כּ, כ, ך	k, ch as in German 'machen'
ל	ל	l
מ, ם	מ	m
נ, ן	נ, ן	n

Printed	Written script	Pronunciation
ס		s
ע		Similar to א
פּ, פ, ף	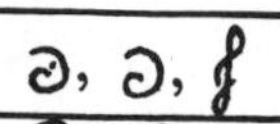	p, f
צ, ץ	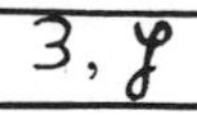	ts
ק		k
ר		r
שׂ, שׁ	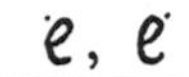	s, sh
תּ, ת	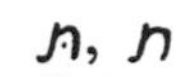	t*

*t (without dāgēš) is pronounced 's' in Ashkenazic.

Table 2. Vowels

	Sign	Pronunciation
Long	◌ָ	a, as in 'father'[1]
	◌ֵ	e, as in 'met'[2]
	◌ִי	i, as in 'machine'
	וֹ	aw, as in 'saw'[3]
	וּ	u, as in 'sure'
Short	◌ַ	a, as in 'father'
	◌ֶ	e, as in 'met'
	◌ִ	i, as in 'hit'
	◌ָ	o, as in 'son'
	◌ֻ	u, as in 'put'

1. Ashkenazic: aw, as in 'saw'
2. " ey, as in 'they'
3. " o, as in 'note'

INDEX TO SUBJECTS